A Welshman Remembers

The story of a Welsh Family, 1938 to the present day...

Robert W.M. Bassett

authorHOUSE®

AuthorHouse™ UK Ltd.
500 Avebury Boulevard
Central Milton Keynes, MK9 2BE
www.authorhouse.co.uk
Phone: 08001974150

First published by AuthorHouse 8/10/2011

ISBN: 978-1-4520-6389-8 (sc)
ISBN: 978-1-4520-6390-4 (hc)
ISBN: 978-1-4567-8525-3 (e)

Dedicated to the memory of my father
David Sydney Bassett who died on May 26th 1986
and of my mother, Doris May Bassett who died April 3rd 2001.

Acknowledgements

I would like to give Thanks to a number of people who
have helped me, during the compiling of these stories,
anecdotes and photographs, over the past years.
My sister Margarette, (Our Peggy) for the many hours and
hard work, that she so willingly gave in the beginning of my
project, when I would send her page upon page of my "longhand
scribble", which she would patiently decipher and put on her
word processor to be sent back and forward by me until it was
exactly what I wanted to say.----------Thank You Peg !!!
I would also like to thank members of my family, and
relatives, who so willingly loaned me many photographs
and many hours of their time, as I would "pester" them for
facts and confirmation ....Thank You Everyone !!!
I would also like to thank my lovely niece Sophie, for so
willingly giving her time and expertise, when I needed it
to prepare the many photographs prior to publication.
And I would also like to thank all those people, too many to
name, who have been involved in my life for all the happiness,
encouragement, and no little amounts of patience, during
all my moments of moodiness .....Thank You all !!!
And last but by no means least to the staff of Authorhouse Publishing
for all their help and advice in seeing this Project becoming reality.

THANK YOU ONE AND ALL.

ROBERT W. M BASSETT
JUNE 2011.

Foreword

When I started the original manuscript my intentions were to produce something different as a birthday gift for mam a couple of years ago, I had no idea how it would turn out and consequently over the ensuing years I have changed the format and increased the contents, and now I am attempting to put these memoirs into chapters to correspond with the various homes and moves that we, as a family have experienced during that time, Mam's 90th birthday was celebrated by a wonderful family get-together at the Masonic Hall in Castleton, on April 27th 1999, though her actual birthday falls on April 21st each year. This function was made possible after a lot of hard work by my sisters, but when it was first suggested I had my doubts because of the amount of travelling it would entail for some of the family. It was a brilliant occasion and I am pleased to say that I have a number of group photographs of the event to treasure.

I have enjoyed compiling these pages and I hope that anyone who reads them will enjoy them as much, but I cannot end without a word of sincere thanks to my sister Peggy for all her efforts and encouragement, and who actually did all the original word processing, re-writing proofs etc and also had the original manuscript bound for me.

At the time when "little sister" was doing all this work, I had no idea just what I was subjecting her to, as I quite happily kept sending her pages of work back, to correct a minor adjustment or spelling error I had made, —but since I have been doing it myself it seems that no matter how many times I check and double check my work I still find spelling mistakes, but I have taught myself the basics on this my trusty computer, and you are now reading my final attempt at completing my work it is very tiring, but it gives me a lot of satisfaction to see it take shape, as I type.

This is also my way of saying Thank You to my family for their support and also ensuring that Mam and Dad will always be remembered in years to come.

My Fathers name was David Sydney Bassett and he was born at "Little Farm" West Nash near Newport, Monmouthshire, on 11th of August 1908 and passed away on 26th of May 1986.

My Mother's maiden name was Doris May Potts and she was born at 61 Magor street, Newport, Monmouthshire on 20th April 1909 and passed away on 3rd of April 2001. Mam always said that her birthday was on April 21st but her birth certificate shows the date as the 20th of that month.

Sadly since I began this manuscript we have lost, first brother in law, Richard Plaisted who died suddenly in his sleep, on Friday, March 18th 2005, and also his wife, my sister Wendy who passed away after a short illness, on Saturday January 21st 2006, they left a son Christopher and a daughter, Elizabeth, who both, thankfully had their families to help them bear their losses. Richard and Wendy are laid to rest in the little country churchyard of St John the Evangelist, in the village of Alvanley, near their home at Helsby in Cheshire. Wendy was always Dad's favourite, possibly because she was his first daughter, after four sons, and also because she did suffer a life-threatening illness when she was very young, so perhaps Dad has used his influence to enable them to be together now, I hope so anyway.!!!

Younger brother Noel's wife Christine, also passed away on December 28th 2006, after battling bravely against cancer, she managed to get to spend a happy Christmas surrounded by her family, and our thoughts went out to all of them, I hope the future holds many happier times for them all.

This manuscript has undergone many changes and adjustments, but I have decided that this will have to be the finished article, I am hoping to complete the task during the coming months, but the days fly by so quickly so I had better press on............

R.W.M.B. May 10th 2007.

Homes along the way.
A summary of our journey.

I was born at "Greenfield" on Nash Road, Newport in 1938, October 15th to be exact, and although I do remember some things about the old home, it is not the purpose of this account, which is to elaborate on our many moves, in order to illustrate just how difficult it was, to keep up with my peers at the various schools that I attended, and to be fair, this problem also applied to my brothers and sisters, to different degrees during their school days.

I was four years old when I began my journey of discovery, at the little village school of Nash, a lengthy walk from my first home at Greenfield, though I remember very little in detail about my time there, we then moved to the village of Llandegveth, which would have been about 1944 when I was about 7, into Brook Cottage, the village was situated between Caerleon and Pontypool, Arthur and David, my elder brothers, were in the big school, Noel and I were in the infants, I must have moved up later, because I vaguely remember Arthur, having a fight with a lad named Leslie Bowditch, at the entrance of "middle school", as we watched, -- I don't recall who "got the decision" though, --Eldest sister Wendy, was born here, and christened in the little Church of St David, (Dewi Sant) which is situated about 100 yards from Brook Cottage, her Godmother was one of the Miss Morgan sisters, who lived alongside the Church.

We then moved to No1 Council Houses, Clytha Road, Llancayo, a cluster of houses, about 2 miles outside Usk, on the road to Abergavenny, in late 1946, and we all enrolled at the village school in Bettws Newydd, --this also entailed a walk of about a mile, to and from school daily, I began in the in the "Little Room" with the younger kids, the teacher was first, Miss Smith, who eventually left to be replaced by the legendary Mr Ball. I remember graduating to the big class, and it was during this period, a most enjoyable part of our young lives, that Dad obtained a job with Mr Trevor Jones at Thornbury Farm, Bettws Newydd, and we moved into the delightful Tump Farm house, I recall as I write, that a certain lady, Mrs Arthur Bull, from the mansion house, visited every family at Christmas, on horseback and delivered a token present, to every child in the village, I qualified to attend King Henry VIII Grammar school, in Abergavenny, by passing the 11plus entrance exam, even though I was only 10 years and 10 months old, in the July of 1949, Arthur must have done likewise, a year or so earlier, David was unlucky, and failed the exam.

My journey to school in Abergavenny entailed going the mile or so to the main Abergavenny—Raglan road to catch the Red and White bus, and I believe, I walked this daily, because at the time Arthur was attending West Mon Grammar School, and there was an understanding in the family, that a new bike would become an accepted "right", at the age of eleven, Arthur collected his, from Bunning's of Usk, but I am sure, that I never received that privilege, and I'm pretty sure also, that David's only arrived at a much later date, and that was while we were living at our sixth home at Pant Cottage, Tylla Lane, St |Mellons.

The reader will appreciate, I hope that this account is compiled by means of a series of deduction, and mental calculations, I recall that for about a term and a half, I went to King Henry's school, because the Headmaster a Mr Newcombe would dictate the history of the school, to the class, and we would copy it into our exercise books, which was not a task I personally enjoyed, I also became great friends with a schoolmate named Phillip Carne, and "stayed over", with his family a number of times, he lived in North Street in the town of Abergavenny.

We were soon on the move again after Dad had gained employment at St Nicholas, a village between Cardiff and Bridgend, in the neighbouring shire of Glamorgan, working for a farmer named Mr Ellis, and we moved into our fifth home, a semi-detached cottage, No 2 Stone Houses, Duffryn Lane, St Nicholas near Cardiff, and eldest brother Arthur had, I believe left school and he also had found employment on a neighbouring farm, called "Dog-Hill farm", working for a Mr Willaims.

I cant remember our sisters ages, Wendy and Peggy, were, I believe still under school age, but David, Noel and I, enrolled at Gladstone Road Elementary school in Barry, until my official transfer came through, and I then enrolled at Barry County High school nearby. This sojourn lasted about a term and a half, I guess, because, we were soon to arrive at our next home, Pant Cottage, in Tylla Lane St Mellons, a whitewashed cottage situated in a narrow lane opposite the St Mellons County Club, and it was here that I experienced my fifth bout of pneumonia and was taken into Llandough Hospital, outside Cardiff and while there also witnessed the spectacle of a jet airliner coming to grief, when a Comet plane crashed in a field close by, this gained extra attention when it was discovered that a large number of rugby personalities were on board. It was also at this time when I had a serious accident to my left hand, which necessitated in my visiting the out patients department of Cardiff Royal Infirmary, twice weekly, which required bus journeys both ways with Mam.

We then moved a couple of miles along the road to Coedkernew, and into a thatched cottage, which was our next home, "The Gardens", at "Berry Hill farm", Coedkernew, where Dad worked for a Mr Robert Parsons, until ill health was to force him into long periods of treatment, at various hospitals, a long tough time for our Mam, -- in every way.

I was just fourteen when we moved to our eighth home, at No ! Bridge Terrace, Michaelstone-y-Fedw, the year, late 1952, not long after the birth of our youngest sister, Carol.-- Dads health had improved a lot and our family life gradually settled down, I would consider our time at this address to be one of the better spells on our travels, but we were to move again, when Mam and Dad decided to swap houses with a friend named, Richards, which took us to No 17 Hillside Crescent, High Cross, Rogerstone, the year about 1956 or 7.

I married the present Mrs Bassett in October 1963, and we rented what was a luxury residential caravan, (the operative word being, "WAS") because it had long since seen better days. This domicile was parked in the corner of a grass paddock, close to the farm house, which we shared with a herd of beef cattle.

I went to work for John Laing Construction Ltd, and was given a council house by the local Magor and St Mellons Urban District Council, at No 1 Elm Close, on the Underwood estate, Llanmartin near Newport, where we lived until September 8th 1977, when we purchased and moved into our newly built house, where I am at this moment seated, in the front bedroom, at No 15 Winchester Close, Pont Ebbw, Newport in South Wales, —busy, actually typing this account, the date today is Wednesday August 4th 2010.

Oh, I have just remembered that in 1958, I went to work for my old, and much valued friends, David and Freda Wyatt, and lived with them for some seven months at Coed-y-Ferm Farm, at Llangwm, a small village, just outside Usk.

According to my calculations that makes 13 homes plus a 4 month stint, in an Army barracks at Deerbolt Camp, Barnard Castle, in Co Durham, with the 60/16 intake, of 1st The Queen's Dragoon Guards in the guise of 23834579 Trooper Bassett R.W.M..

I am fast approaching my 72nd Birthday, so I really don't envisage ANY more moves, but it has been fun and very interesting getting HERE.

Stately Homes of the Bassett Dynasty.

"Little Farm", West Nash, near Newport,
Monmouthshire.

"Greenfield" Nash Road, Newport, Monmouthshire.

"Brook Cottage", Llangegveth, near Newport,
Monmouthshire.

No1, Clytha Road, Llancayo, near Usk,
Monmouthshire.

"Tump Farm", Bettws-Newydd, Near
Usk, Monmouthshire.

No2, Stone Houses, Duffryn Lane, St Nicholas,
Near Cardiff, Glamorgan.

"Pant Cottage", Tylla Lane, St Mellons, near,
Cardiff, Glamorgan.

"The Gardens", Berry Hill, Coedkernew, near
Newport, Monmouthshire.

No1, Bridge Terrace, Michaelstone-y-Fedw, near
Newport Monmouthshire.

No17, Hillside Crescent, High- Cross Lane,
Rogerstone, Monmouthshire.

"The Caravan", Court Farm, Caldicot, near
Chepstow, Monmouthshire.

No1, Elm Close, Llanmartin, near Newport
Monmouthshire.

15 Winchester Close, Newport, Gwent.

Robert W.M. Bassett.

Wednesday, August 4th 2010.

Chapter One

My Earliest Recollections

My earliest memories take me back over sixty- six years to when I was about four years old, we were living in the house where I was born on October 15th 1938. The house was called "Greenfield", a large detached stone built building on Nash Road on the outskirts of Newport, in the county of Monmouthshire, South Wales, mam and dad had rented part of the house from an old lady named Mrs Williams, and I remember numerous occasions, of hiding in the cupboard of a large Welsh dresser, and eating brown sugar, a particular favourite of mine, to this day, which belonged to the aforementioned lady.

I had not yet started school, but I recall standing on the bottom rung of the white five barred front gate, looking through the rails as my two elder brothers, Arthur and David, set off to walk the mile or so, to the small school in the village of Nash. When I eventually started there, I remember the teachers name was Miss Greenway.

The house was, I believe, actually owned by our close neighbours, a farming family named Attewell, who lived in the adjoining property, a farm called "The Lakes", which was separated from us, by a rene or ditch, which was usually fairly stagnant, and often dried up during the hot summer months.

Our Uncle Charlie and Aunty Betty Griffiths, Mam's sister, would often come to visit us from the Corporation Road area of Newport, and Uncle Charlie, who had rather a mischievous streak, one day, whilst on leave from the Army, decided that he could leap across the aforementioned ditch, and without further ado, proceeded to try, to do just that, but unfortunately for him, this feat proved impossible, and as a result he landed some way short of his objective, knee deep in ink black, slimy mud, fully dressed in his immaculate, Army uniform.

It was about this time, that I had what was the first, of five bouts of pneumonia, and my last recollection of life at "Greenfield", was that of sitting in the cab of a removal van, wrapped in a blanket, as we left the old house, and were on our way to our new home, in the village of Llandegveth, near Caerleon, some five miles from Newport, where Dad had secured employment with a Mr Joe Shepherd, who farmed the large "Ty Capten Farm in that village.

Dad, being the son of a farmer, was naturally drawn to the life of agricultural toil, which was hard, low paid and invariably led to our family living in a variety of "tied cottages", as Dad, like so many other farm workers, struggling with the problems of growing families and static wages, searched for better conditions.

Our move to Llandegveth, was the first of what was to be an often repeated event, when we moved into our new home, named, "Brook Cottage", I was about six years old, and I remember that it was here, that I grew addicted to all kinds of fruit, such as the apples and pears, in fact, everything that grew in our new orchard, adjoining our home, and I would sit, either in, or under the trees for hours, eating, until eventually, all the trees were bare.

My brothers and I, attended Caerleon Endowed school, younger brother Noel and I, were in the infants, and, as such were required to go to bed in the afternoons on camp beds erected in the classrooms, these were tubular and canvas contraptions. No one told me that we would be packed off home at the required time, with the result that I used to lie rigid, terrified, that the bus with Arthur and David on board, would go without us, and that Noel and I would be there all night.

It was also at Brook Cottage that I first began to think that "Father

Christmas" seemed to work in a strange way. Let me elaborate, in her teenage years Mam, had worked for, and become life-long friends with her employers, a Captain and Mrs Hillman, who lived at "The Anchorage" No 100, on Corporation Road, Newport, and consequently, each Christmas, Mam would send a couple of us kids, on the bus to collect "the presents" from Mrs Hillman's house. These were gifts kindly given by this good lady, to help Mam during the days of "rationing", in the years following the second World War, and were usually things which Mrs Hillman's children had finished playing with, and that they had received the previous year, but although our presents were usually second-hand, I can vividly remember the days leading up to Christmas were tremendously exciting, none of us were ever disappointed with our Christmas presents.

Brook Cottage, was situated in a wooded area, with a single track lane running past the front gate, with a brook of clear water adjacent to it, this brook crossed the lane at forty five degrees, some fifty yards further along, and it was necessary to be quite nimble footed to get across the water by hopping from one stepping stone to the next to reach the other side. During wet spells, the brook would increase in volume and on one occasion, I remember we had found a long tin bath, which to our delight, seemed ideal to use as a boat, brother David spent quite a while, trying to persuade me to climb aboard, as he stood on the bank and struggled to hold it, as it bobbed about in the swirling muddy current, thank goodness, I resisted his powers of persuasion because I'm sure I would have drowned had I climbed aboard.

To get to school we would go to the top of the steep hill, where we would be picked up by the school bus, which was a canvas covered charabanc, owned by a company in Caerleon, Mark Howells Ltd. Now this vehicle was extremely noisy and could be heard for miles, as it wheezed it's way around the narrow lanes towards us, as we stood in a small group hoping against hope, that it would not arrive, and that we would have a days holiday instead of having to go to school, but I cant remember ever having our wish come true.!!!

3

Around the corner from Brook cottage, is a long white cottage, which was at that time divided into two dwellings, and actually had an adjoining door between the two living rooms, our school-friend David Harris lived in one and I often wondered if they ever had the urge to open this door when the other family were away. Just a bit further up the hill was The Farmer's Arms inn, and one of the delights for us kids, was the large heap of coloured bottle tops, which had built up in the yard outside. These bottle tops were all different colours and made terrific "badges", David my brother, often used to install himself as a "army captain", and would march me up and down the field, at the rear of our house, stopping occasionally to award me a decoration, consisting of one of these "badges", or a "medal", which was actually a twig with leaves attached, as a token of reward, for some act of bravery or such like, in the course of duty, which I had "achieved", during these marches, —he would poke the twigs through the material of my pullover, and by the end of our game, I would be well decorated with twigs and leaves, --Mam wasn't too pleased to see the state of my garments though!!!

I had become interested in tractors, and would seize every opportunity to ride with Alan Shepherd, on the David Brown tractor, which actually had a double seat, enabling a passenger to sit alongside the driver. I was absolutely enthralled by this wonderful machine, which was a light fawn colour, but was later sprayed into its usually known colour, bright red, . While we lived at Brook Cottage we would take turns to walk up the steep hill, cross the lane, and then the two fields to Shepherds farm house to collect a large jug of fresh milk, for Mam, when it was my turn to go, I would, on the return journey take large gulps of milk until the jug would be considerably less than full, whereupon, I would resolve this shortfall, by topping it up, at the cows drinking trough, on the side of the path which I passed as I journeyed homewards, --no-one seemed to notice the considerably diluted milk, but I personally hated skimmed milk until quite recently.

On another occasion I had instructions from Mam to go to the butchers in Caerleon, after school, and collect a large piece of corned beef and to bring it home, -- on reflection I must have been only about nine years of age at that time, I did as instructed, but in my early years, I always seemed to have a ravenous appetite, and the temptation was too much, and I resorted to breaking off little bits of the corn beef and eating it, until eventually, I reached a point where it hardly seemed worth while taking the remainder home, so I thought I might just as well eat it, I knew that I would have a warm reception when I arrived home, anyway, !!!! But seriously, I never liked corn beef for years, afterwards.

Brook Cottage was a detached rough cast covered house, and as a part of job concession, Dad was given the run of the large orchard, and kept many chickens and ducks, he obtained a large wooden packing case, which was designed to contain four army Jeeps, during transportation overseas, by boat. These crates stood about four feet high, and had a small hinged door at one corner. I remember travelling on the David Brown tractor, with Dad and Alan Shepherd, towing a four wheeled trailer, to collect it, although I'm not sure, but I think it came from Granny Bassett's at Nash, though I cant recall what happened to it afterwards, I do remember it was extremely dark inside, Dad used it to house chickens in the field at the rear of Brook Cottage.

In the village of Llandegveth, lived an old lady named Miss Whitlock, who would give us stale cakes if we called on her at any time, on one occasion I can still remember, that while we were playing nude in the tree lined brook, which ran through the field near our house, she came tripping across to see us, I didn't have time to get my clothes on, I recall that it seemed like an eternity that she peered into the brook, as I cowered, trying to hide my embarrassment, as the water seemed to get colder and colder !!!!

We had a friend named David Harris, who lived close by and my school-friend was a boy named Arthur Tucker, who came from a farming family, and lived about a mile or so away, and, who incidentally, I met years later in the local cattle market, amazingly he also remembered our time at Caerleon Infants school, particularly the camp bed scenario.

I used to take every opportunity to ride on the David Brown tractor with Alan Shepherd, and whenever I could find where he was working, which wasn't difficult, because the sound of the tractor was easy to hear, in those days, due to lack of traffic around the roads, and I recall going into the fields with him on the tractor and a trailer, and I guess it must have been during the winter time, he would be taking fodder to the stock, when we had arrived at the field, he would put the tractor in gear and jump off, get onto the trailer and toss the fodder to the stock, I would slide across the seat to the drivers side, and would "drive" the tractor as it" crawled" in low gear around the field, until he had finished and climbed back into the seat and took control again-- I can still visualize the shiny steering wheel with the smooth black centre, and also the gauge on the front bonnet which had a hand, and black red and green markings, I later learned that this was a temperature gauge, I guess that I must have been about eight or nine years old at that time.

At other times when he was ploughing, Alan Shepherd would remove the back rest off the seat and replace in a different position so that it formed an arm rest, close to the mudguards on both sides of the tractor was a lever, these were actually the independent brake levers, for each rear wheel, I guessed that they WERE a type of brake, and would give the lever a "tug" now and then, but it never seemed to have any effect, much to my disappointment!!!! I was enthralled by the two gear levers which were mounted on the raised part of the tractor between me and Mr Shepherd, one slightly longer than the other, thirty odd years later, I had the pleasure of actually using one of these David Brown tractors at a farm situated at Penylan, near Bassaleg, belonging to a farmer named Mr Donald Cawley, which gave me tremendous enjoyment, I still get a buzz every time I see these tractors.

I have on a number of occasions been back to the village of Llandegveth, and enjoyed eating lunch at the aforementioned Farmers Arms Inn which does a very tasty line in catering, but the old Brook Cottage has been completely demolished and replaced by a substantially new modern dwelling.

Chapter Two

Llancayo, and Tump Farm, Bettws Newydd

On leaving Brook Cottage, we then moved into No 1 The Council Houses, Clytha Road Llancayo, , which was the first of a block of eight terraced houses situated some two miles outside the small market town of Usk, on the road to Abergavenny. We were out in the country again, and on reflection I can understand why we enjoyed life so much, because even today with the countryside lacerated by motorways and suchlike. it is still a beautiful area.

The river Usk passed close-by, and during warm weather, we would strip off and jump in, until one summer an outbreak of Infantile Paralysis occurred, and we were warned not to do this any more, we were standing on the riverbank, discussing this strange sounding phenomenon, and we decided there and then, by mutual consent, that this paralysis thing must be the numerous bubbles we could see floating past!!!! It was also at Llancayo that I learned to ride a bicycle, or at least how to stay upright in motion, unfortunately, I couldn't master the art of dismounting and, as a result, I used to ride rather precariously along until I spotted an inviting area of roadside whereupon I would serenely topple sideways to the ground, unfortunately, it was also at this time that I discovered nettles, and usually ended up with arm and legs, covered in itchy pimples caused by the aforementioned nettles.

When we moved into our home at Llancayo, we were sent to Bettws Newydd school, which entailed a nice walk of about a mile and a half each way, but we never seemed to notice the distances we were required to walk in those far off days, in fact, at our previous home at Brook Cottage, at trip to see our Granny Bassett at Little Farm, West Nash, meant that we would first walk the two miles to the main Caerleon/Usk road, where we would catch a bus to Newport, then we would catch another bus to the Lyaght's Institute on Corporation Road, and then walk the mile or so to the very end, and clamber up onto the rail track, and walk alongside the rail-lines through the grounds of the Aluminium Works, until we eventually came to Granny's farm, which was situated exactly where the big Uskmouth Power station now stands, so the reader will understand that we became well used to long treks on foot.

The council house where were we were now living in, had no water supply when we first moved in, but this was put right soon afterwards, but unfortunately the workmen forgot to ensure that all the taps were turned off, and as a result, when the main supply was turned on, the ground floor became flooded, which raised the new block flooring in our front room, I don't ever remember the room being usable during our term of residence.

Dad was working for Mr Evan Williams, who farmed Llancayo Farm, which was only a five minute walk from our home, and in the summer we would often play football, in the field close-by, during one game Dad and Mam joined in, Dad who had in his youth played a lot of football for his village team of Nash United, as a goal-keeper, unleashed a tremendous kick, the ball flew like a rocket, caught Mam, with a terrific thud, and flattened her, she was out cold, but thank goodness, soon recovered.

Some of our school-friends lived near us, Christopher(Tubby) Davies lived in the white cottage near-by, and was in the habit of sucking his thumb, particularly in moments of stress, I used to see him, quite often, during my working visits to Newport Cattle Market, and he is quite a well established local farmer, but even now I often notice him having a quick suck of his trusty thumb, in moments of forgetfulness, although he must be in his mid sixties now. Raymond Griffiths, a little lad, who had rather a severe speech impediment, had an elder brother named Vernon, who promised me a pair of his old football boots, as soon as he could unearth them from his garden shed, ---I just could not wait to get my hands on these wonderful things---I had only ever seen a pair in a shop window, and each time I went to call for Raymond, I would ask, eagerly, had he found them, until one day he gave me one boot, --now Vernon, was at that time much older than us kids, and this boot was huge, but I didn't care, I was so "chuffed" to have football boots(or boot), I badgered him unmercifully to give me the other one, but I can't ever remember receiving it.

Raymond got knocked down by a car and was rushed to hospital seriously injured, and I remember how shocked I was when he eventually returned home, with his head all shaved and bandaged. Dad's employer had three children, John, Margaret and David, they also attended Bettws Newydd school, and walked the journey both ways

Mr Evan Williams, Dad's old employer, passed away in May2007, at the age of 93, and Raymond who now lives at Pontnewynydd, is the secretary of the local football leagues, though as yet, I haven't met or spoken to him for many years.

It was at Llancayo that I remember being put into a local fête, dressed or rather undressed as a boxer, and this obviously gave me my interest in the sport in later years..

While we were living at Llancayo, we would often walk the few miles into the little town of Usk to watch the local football team, Usk Town play their "home" games on their pitch, appropriately named "The Island" due to its close proximity the River Usk, and it was here that we found our first sporting "idols", and used to "look up" to such sporting icons as Stan York, the centre forward, and Spencer Kear, the goalkeeper, who in our eyes, were the Alan Shearer and Peter Shilton of our era, after the game we would wait patiently in Usk for the arrival of the South Wales Football Argus, for ages, the thought never seemed to enter our heads that the paper wouldn't be printed for a long time after our game had finished, we just waited patiently and some weeks, if we were lucky and could afford it, we would have fish and chips.---A treat!!!

I have quite recently on a number of occasions, been back to Usk to watch the football team in action, and enjoyed the experience, though I was a little surprised to see that they now play in a smart green and white hooped kit, and own their own mini-bus, probably sponsored by a local company which they use to travel to away games around the county..I always thought they played in blue and white, but there again, my memory can play tricks, I suppose.

Half way between Usk and Llancayo were tea-rooms, known locally as "The Cycling Club" purely because, rarely a day passed without there being lots of bicycles lying against the roadside, as their owners were obtaining refreshments inside, I often wonder what it would be like these days, --I've no doubt that the aforementioned bikes would surely need to be under lock and key, but in those far-off days they were not!.

Our next move was only as far as the next village, of Bettws Newydd where we moved into the quaintly named Tump Farm house, after dad had obtained work with a Mr Trevor Jones, who farmed Thornbury Farm, situated on the road leading from the Abergavenny road at Chain Bridge, to Bettws Newydd, I believe the farm was part of the larger Brynderwyn Court Estate, owned by Mrs and Major Arthur Bull, who were amongst some of the wealthiest people in the country back in the 1940's.

This is a beautiful area of countryside, predominantly wooded, and quite hilly, I consider it one of the nicest places we have had the good fortune to have lived. Our house was set well away from the roads, and was the original farm house, The house was situated on the corner of a cobbled quadrangle of buildings, and was joined onto a large stone barn, a tractor shed along one side of the yard, a row of calf pens and a pigsty or two, led along the other two sides of the yard to where a five barred gate was hung. Outside, what was the back door of our house, was a cobbled bailey, with a retaining wall, with steps leading up to a grass field, on the opposite side was another wall, with a small gate and steps leading down, into the aforementioned farm yard. The bailey actually joined onto another stone building, a stable adjoining a high Dutch barn, where we had several ropes fixed to the high girders in the roof which we used as swings, and for climbing.

Mam being town, born and raised, had taken to country life and, I believe enjoyed every minute, and on the occasion of a family trek to see either Granny Bassett or Granny Potts it was not unusual for Dad to get ready, and then to say to Mam that he was "just popping to see that the calves were OK" or some such thing, and to disappear to return some time later slightly the worse for his efforts, but Mam seemed to realise that these moments were all part and parcel of being a farming wife.

One other thing which we kids were not so keen on, was when Mam would give us a fork from the cutlery drawer, and tell us to weed between the cobbles of the bailey, outside the back door, she liked to keep the place weed free.

The front of our house, led onto a large garden, in which Dad had planted many red, and black currant bushes, as well as many raspberry canes, which I used to enjoy raiding when the fruit was fit to eat. The house and several of the buildings were lower than the ground level, on the one side and I remember that brother David, who was very keen on gardening had cultivated a small area high up in the one corner against the side of the house, and grew many lettuces etc, where as I, being eager but not too conversant with the technical side of gardening, had settled for a small area in the wood adjoining the garden, and had planted orange nasturtiums, not knowing that this species of plant would grow and rapidly encroach everywhere. I thought it was down to my expertise and possible new found gardening skills!!

To get to our school in the village of Bettws Newydd, we would climb the steps from the bailey, and make our way across to two fields to the lane, where incidentally the new Thornbury Farm house now stands, we would then make our way along the narrow lane, to the village, where there was the Post Office, the home of the Brookes family, then we would pass the Black Bear Inn and continue down the small hill to the little school, which stood opposite a white painted rough cast house, which was the home of the Phillips family, the twins Victor and Vivien, and their two sisters Rosemary and Molly.

It was during my time at this school that I became aware of the attentions of Lavinia Coyle, a classmate, who was a plump girl with long pig-tails and a toothy smile, accentuated by dimples in each chubby cheek, and it seemed that no matter which way I looked, she would be there, just looking and smiling, --I escaped the attentions of dear Lavinia when I sat, and passed the eleven plus exam, even though I was actually only ten years and ten months old, I thereby qualified to attend the grammar school.

The head teacher at Bettws Newydd school was Mrs Rees, a large lady, who we named "Ole Ma Rees", but for the early years my time was spent in the "little room" with the infants, where we were under the watchful eye of a youngish Mr Ball, who rode a bicycle, and always had a blue ruck sack over his shoulders. One day during lessons he asked the class, "who would like to be an engineer when you grow up?", without hesitation I put my hand up, I had no idea what an engineer was, but it seemed like a good idea, at the time, !!------whereupon he gave me a large volume and told me to read it.

When I opened the book, I was immediately confronted with what was complete gobbledegook to me, with lots of plans and diagrams, and long words which were obviously "way above my head" but each afternoon from then on, Mr Ball would be taking the class, and I would be told, "Get on with your book, Robert"---I would then sit, head bowed, supposedly engrossed, reading, when actually I had no idea what I was looking at !!

The classes were made up of many characters, there was Billy(Spud) Taylor, Donald(Ducklow) Powell, Leslie Watkins, Sheila Brookes,

Charlie and Yvonne Murray, Lavinia of course, Melba and her brother Tony and Michael Evans, a lad who always seemed to have items or information with which to astound and amaze us, one such article was his "everlasting pen" which would "write for ever and never needed filling", this was, of course a ball point pen, new to us, because being so far out in the country and newspapers being practically non existent in our neck of the woods we were easily convinced.

Of course, Kenneth Jones, the son of Dad's employer, was also in our class, as were John, Margaret and David Williams from Llancayo, Dad's former employer, as was Christopher (Tubby) Davies, , and on reflection, I guess it would be fair to say, that this was the probable favourite of all our homes, the countryside was certainly the most beautiful then, and still is.

I have since visited Bettws Newydd on many occasions and also been made most welcome by Kenneth and his lovely wife Frances at their beautiful Thornbury Farm House, and was also taken by Ken to visit Brynderwyn House, nearby which is now owned by a consultant/surgeon Mr Peter Williams, but the manor house has been turned into luxury private apartments, —incidentally Mr Williams operated on my left hand in 2005 at the Royal Gwent Hospital, though he also has a big house in Stow Park Circle Newport, Tump Farm is now owned by Mr Thomas Bird, the managing director of "The Bird Group" of companies, a large scrap metal combine, and the old place has been extensively modernised, and is now a very attractive modern home.

It certainly was a lovely experience to go back and to meet such nice welcoming people.

Chapter Three

The things we did back then...........

It was while we were at Tump Farm, that Dad reared a huge pig, which actually weighed some twenty two score, which by modern standards was enormous, the animal was slaughtered by the butcher, in the cobbled yard outside our house, and I can still recall how it squealed as it died, afterwards it was covered by a pile of clean straw, which was set alight, and allowed to burn in order to remove the bristles from the skin of the animal, . The carcass was then cut from top to bottom into two halves, the skin scrubbed, and placed on two stone slabs in the dairy of our house and covered in a mixture of salt and salt petre, and left to cure for the required time. Then came the chitterlings, which were actually the stomach of the animal, which were placed in a large tin bath to be cleansed by means of a series of water treatments, all carried out manually, which I will not elaborate upon, suffice to say that it involved a jug and a lot of water, and a lot of hard work, and I have no doubt that it was extremely thorough, I am sure was equal to anything done by the experts of today, and the food produced by these seemingly primitive methods, was invariably more tasty than the pathetic offerings on sale in modern supermarkets.

After the two sides had lain for the necessary time, for the salt etc to do its job, they were hung using two strong hooks from the dairy ceiling, and eventually Dad started cutting however much of the particular meat etc, Mam would require for the meal in question, and this procedure continued until eventually only the ham of the hind leg remained, and it never ceases to amaze me, that in this modern world of sell-by dates etc, there appears to be many more case of food poisoning and the like, than there were then, I wonder why?.

Each year, the days leading up to Christmas, were taken up with Mam and Dad busily preparing poultry, reared by Dad, for distribution to the many neighbours and other folk who had placed orders for them in the weeks leading up to Christmas, this entailed killing, plucking, and "dressing" the birds, but due to the lack of electricity and heating, this task was carried out in our living room, and it was not unusual to find the hearth deep in feathers, with prepared and partly prepared ducks and chickens, occupying every available space, and if you were not careful a feather or two would often settle on ones sandwich of jam or syrup.!!

In today's world, of television, videos, stereos and computer games, youngsters often complain of boredom, and having "nothing to do", yet before electricity and every day facilities which are common place now, our only entertainment, apart from cinemas, was our "wireless". This was powered by a dry battery and an accumulator, --a glass acid filled power pack which had to be "charged" up similar to a car battery, which had to be done at regular intervals, but would usually begin to "run down" at the most inopportune moments, it was quite usual to see our family crowded close to our trusty wireless, straining to hear the end of "the big fight", "Dick Barton," or "Mrs Dale's Diary", but even though we were a large family of four boys and three girls, I cant ever remember being bored or having nothing to do.

On one occasion, being "football mad", we discovered it was possible to buy studs for football boots, and by knocking them into the soles of our ordinary school lace up boots, we could simulate our soccer idols, with "proper boots", but due to the heel on our ordinary boots being extended somewhat by the one inch stud, it did tend to pitch one forward somewhat, and it soon became apparent that Mam wasn't too thrilled by our treatment of our school footwear either.!!

We did have some terrific "matches" though, although we were short in numbers, Arthur "was" Manchester City, David "was" Derby County, and I "was" Aston Villa, but looking back I am not sure how we would have coped with the number of substitutes allowed in the modern game.!!

When we were kids, hairdressers were unheard of, except for the legendary Ollie Ireland, who was the coiffure expert in Bettws Newydd, but in our family, Dad would take care of this task, using whatever implements were available, and he became adept, using the hand shears, which were used for shearing sheep, but these implements were not designed for intricate detail, such as fringes or neck trimming, and it was usually very apparent that our hair had been cut at home.

On one occasion Arthur had read that hairdressers often used a singeing technique, and he persuaded me to let him "do" mine, and that he could do it to a satisfactory standard, so I agreed and he proceeded, using a number of boxes of matches, !!! some time later, he HAD eradicated all the uneven lengths which usually signified home -cut hair, but for ages afterwards my head resembled a mass of shrivelled ends and an aroma of burnt hair followed me around, despite numerous washes and combing. !!

I was by now attending a grammar school, and my hair style, or lack of it, was usually the centre of many unkind "cuts" from my classmates, although in hindsight, and after studying the modern trends, I was a trend setter, way ahead of my time.!!

Some of the most enjoyable and memorable times of my childhood, were our years at the last three aforementioned homes, and it was here that our whole family seemed to get involved wherever Dad was working, let me explain, Dad was primarily, an experienced cowman and herdsman, and as such usually did his job without the need of supervision, such as the milking and care of all the stock, morning and evening, but would often "lend a hand" with the other workers during harvest etc, which is where we the family would be allotted small tasks to assist, such as being delegated to the fields to "stook" sheaves of corn upright after they were discharged from the "reaper and binder" which was the forerunner of the modern combine harvester.

This was done after the corn was first cut, to allow it to dry and ripen, until it could be transported to the barns. This operation was followed by "thrashing", done by a large noisy machine and was an extremely dusty job, and invariably we would be given jobs to assist. One was to rake cavings and husks from the chute, as they were discharged from the "thrashing drum", to do this, one would be armed with a long handled wooden rake and be required to stand up to waist height in the chaff and to endeavour to keep the chute clear as the waste came out in a continuous stream from the machine. At "knocking off" time, usually at nightfall in the summer months, we would go home, and even though we had already made every effort to rid ourselves of all traces of straw and dust, outside, invariably during undressing for bed, it would emerge from every nook cranny and orifice of ones person, to form a conspicuous "circle" on the floor of the bedrooms.

It is worth stopping to consider the following facts, there would be at this time, at least four boys and possibly one girl in our little "brood", and the mind boggles when you think that there would be at least three of us spreading the remnants of our days toil, on the bedroom floor, as well as Dad in the other bedroom, remember this was also before vacuum-cleaners had been invented, Mam must have had to work "her socks off" to clean the house in those far-off days.

It was hard work at times, but in hindsight, those days were enjoyable as well, particularly during harvest, when Mrs Trevor Jones would bring a large hamper, full of sandwiches, tea, cakes and lemonade down to the field where we were working and everyone would gather round for a large sumptuous picnic tea on the hayfield.

Mr Jones, Dad's employer also had a brand new David Brown tractor, which was kept in the shed situated in the corner of the yard close to our house, I used to spend hours sitting in the driving seat of this wonderful machine "driving it", although there were no windows in this building, and it was rather dark too.!!.

To go back some years, at Brook Cottage, Llandegveth, German prisoners of war, were at the time being held at holding camps around the country, and would be sent out to farms under supervision, to work, and Mr Joe Shepherd, had two such individuals working at Ty Capten Farm, their names were Martin Roscher and Conrad Mueller, and over the ensuing months they became well liked friends of our family, and even spent Christmas with us at Brook Cottage, I vaguely recall that Martin had a nasty accident, when a tractor ran over his leg, years later, —they also were repatriated home to Germany later.

It was also at Brook Cottage that Arthur and David, hit upon the idea, of selling fruit around the village, and consequently loaded up their home-made four "wheeled bogey", and set off around the village, eventually arriving at the top of the hill leading back down to our house, with their empty truck, which they decided to sit in, and ride down the steep hill, but unbeknown to them a horse and trolley, was unloading at the Farmers Arms, with the horse standing across the lane grazing on the bank, meanwhile Arthur and David were just setting off and building "a nice head of steam" on their homeward run, only to suddenly encounter the horse blocking their path, having no means of halting their headlong progress, they ducked their heads low and hurtled straight under the belly of the startled animal. To make matters worse the fruit that they were so industriously trading around the neighbourhood belonged to Mr Shepherd, Dad's boss, who actually owned our orchard.

To get back to Bettws Newydd, having no dining facilities at the school, we used to take our sandwiches to school in "dried milk tins" which were large and were affixed to baler twine to enable us to sling them over our shoulders, in the manner of a school satchel, which were out of our "price range", and each morning we would receive the complementary school milk, which came in third of a pint bottle, which the teacher would warm by placing them, half immersed, in a bucket of water, and heated on the oil heater, at the front of the class room, --I loved this treat.

Because there were no sports facilities at the school, the only physical education we received was when or if someone brought a football to school.

We did however arrange and play a couple of football matches that I remember, one was against the neighbouring village school of Llanfair Kilgeddin, which we won easily, and the other was against Gwehelog which we lost, but losing that one came as no surprise because we had to walk to both games, and the one at Gwehelog was a good three miles away. Footballs in those early days were made of leather and were very water absorbent, on that occasion I remember, kicking the ball was like kicking a boulder, which come to think of it, was probably where I broke a bone in my right foot, which gives me a lot of pain, even today.

One morning at school, we discovered that there was a "meet of the local fox-hounds, so my brothers and I along with two or three classmates, decided that we would follow them, away we went directly after the morning break, and had a tremendous day chasing along the lanes and fields, with wild shouts of "Tally Ho", and straining our necks to catch a glimpse of the hounds, or the red coats of the huntsmen, until our stomachs told us it was time to return to the school, to collect our belongings. We had judged that "Ole Ma Rees", would surely have gone home, and that only Bessie Taylor, "Billy spuds", sister, who cleaned the school, would be there, WRONG!!!.......we could see the formidable figure of our Headmistress seated by the fireside in the empty classroom.

We decided that we would hide in the empty chicken-house, in the adjoining field, where we could see when she left to go home, but after waiting, for what seemed like ages, we all agreed that she didn't seem to WANT to go home, so we all went our separate ways and had to make up stories to our parents, for not having our coats etc with us, when we eventually arrived at our respective homes. In hindsight, I think our

Headmistress was probably sat worrying about the whereabouts of a number of her pupils.!!

On another occasion, the school was agog with the news that Tommy Heath and Ken Wainwright, cousins who lived at the lodge of Brynderwyn Court, the home of Major and Mrs Bull, the owners of the large country estate, had run away from home, and although this WAS big news for some time, I being only about nine years old, at the time, didn't and come to that, still don't know, where, or if, they were eventually found, --but it did seem very exciting at the time, --but there again, I thought that the"Just William" book was an autobiography.!!

Chapter Four

On the move, ...Abroad, ...
and Back again.!!!

It was time for us to be on the move again, and though I am not sure how it came about, Dad had found work in the neighbouring county of Glamorgan, and we moved into our new home at No2 Stone Houses, Duffryn Lane, in the village of St Nicholas which is situated about four miles from Cardiff on the road to Bridgend. We moved into the second of a pair of semi-detatched houses, and our next door neighbour was an old man named Mr Ward, who soon became "Ole Wardie" to us kids.

My memory is pretty vague about this episode of our life, but I have since discovered that Dad was employed by a farmer named Ellis, who often used to take brother David to watch Cardiff rugby in action at the old Cardiff Arms Park. Peggy and I visited St Nicholas recently and had rather a pleasant chat with some of the folk who still live there, our old home is now a rather desirable property too.

Due to having to get official "transfer notification" to move from one grammar school to another, I had to enrol with David and Noel at Gladstone Road Elementary school in Barry, but later changed to Barry County High school, I was never very happy there because pupils were actually only allowed to speak the Welsh language during school hours, which to the vast majority this wasn't a problem, but to me it was, and so, very soon I became a loner, and if that wasn't bad enough the school had a half day each Wednesday, but I having not yet obtained a season ticket, wasn't able to use the public service bus, to get home, had to wait till 4.15pm for the school bus.

On two occasions, I decided to walk home, and my journey was along the Barry to Cardiff road to Culverhouse Cross, on the outskirts of the city, then left up the long incline called the Tumble, through Bonvilston, and on to St Nicholas and home, I was still only eleven years old, and had heard that if one waved a thumb at passing motorists, you would very often be offered a lift, but I, being rather shy, didn't "like to do this", so I hit on the idea of limping painfully, in the hope that they would take pity on me and offer me the lift, but although I tried this brilliant ruse on a number of occasions, I never once got a lift, I'm relieved to say that, though I quite liked the village, we were soon on the move again and eventually moved into Tylla Lane near Castleton, half way between Cardiff and Newport, home territory again!!.

Our new home, Pant Cottage, a long low whitewashed rough cast cottage, in a narrow lane, was actually what seemed like a converted bungalow, because though there were second story bedrooms, they were tent shaped, with no walls and we had a sky light window to partly relieve the claustrophobic element, caused by the roof being so low.--the bedrooms were actually the attic space.

Dad had obtained work with a Mr Thomas who farmed the adjoining Pant Farm and I soon enrolled at Bassaleg Grammar school and travelled to and from school on Western welsh buses which ran along the main Cardiff/Newport road close by.

It was here that I had the last of my five bouts of pneumonia, which led to my first hospital spell, when I was admitted to Llandough Hospital, and it was here during that stay, that I actually witnessed the sad, though spectacular sight of a chartered airliner, come to grief in a field close to the hospital, as it was returning from Dublin with rugby personalities and pressmen on board after an International match in 1950.

Shortly after I was discharged, brother Arthur, who was always one for a laugh, decided to play a prank on me, I had been home only a short while, confined to bed, wallowing in self pity, more than anything, and enjoying being the centre of attention, from Mam, --he crawled under my bed, and by arching his back, gently raised and lowered my mattress, with me on it-- I had been lying there some time and I began to realise that there was a strange sensation occurring, but wasn't quite sure what it was, I thought, I AM ill, what on earth?-------with that I raised myself onto all fours on the bed, and peered underneath in the gloom........it was pretty dark by now, and I thought I could see …..a ghostly white hand.......and without further ado, proceeded to YELL at the top of my voice, for Mam !!.

The sound of my yelling, brought Mam and several other members of the family to see what on earth all the noise was about, -------Arthur, emerged, grinning broadly, from under my bed, and was told in no uncertain terms by Mam to go downstairs and let me sleep. or words to that effect!!

Dad, who was an experienced cowman and stockman, worked long hours without supervision, but though Mam accepted this, she frowned upon Dad working on a Sunday, other than connected with the stock, but one Sunday, with the skies looking doubtful, Mr Thomas asked Dad if he would assist them to clear a field of hay, before the rain came. Dad agreed and the hay was being brought in, and stored in the big Dutch barn, where they were using a "hay-grab", which was a metal claw-like contraption, operated by a series of ropes and pullies, attached by a long rope to a shire horse, which was capable of lifting huge quantities of hay and raising it up onto the rick where Dad was busy building the rick.

I watched this process for quite a while, and slowly an idea began to form in my mind, that if I grabbed the rope at a certain time, and hung on, I too would be lifted onto the high rick where Dad was working, so making sure, not to be noticed, I waited till what I thought was an opportune moment, and grabbed the rope..............I had expected to be hoisted aloft, but I got a terrible shock, as I was yanked violently sideways, and my hands were rapidly drawn into the deep groove of a round pulley, where a rope passing through it, quickly and painfully lacerated my fingers, and tore the skin from my hands.

The terrible pain, caused me to scream out and caught the attention of the workers, who immediately rushed to my rescue, and I was then whisked away to Cardiff Royal infirmary, where I received treatment, and for the next eight months I was taken twice weekly by Mam, where my hands were treated by a series of having my hands bathed in wax until the skin returned, but unfortunately, the tendons in my fingers had been damaged, and I can no longer bend or straighten my fingers, which led to complications in later years when I was boxing.

Incidentally, the resulting injuries of this accident, were improved upon by the surgeon the Mr Peter Williams, mentioned in the previous chapter, in his capacity at the Royal Gwent Hospital, who I happened to meet while undergoing an examination for another ailment, not long ago in 2008. I now have recovered the use of my left hand, or at least 98% of the use of it.

It was also at Pant Cottage, that elder brother David received his promised new bicycle, which was a terrific green colour, and was a"Phillips" make, --Arthur had received his, a black "Hurcules" some years earlier, during our sojourn at Tump Farm, David loved his new bike and used to spend hours cleaning and polishing it, till it shone, he would literally ride for mile after mile, and the first thing he would do, on arriving home, would be to clean his beloved bike.!!

Another occasion, I remember vividly, I had been playing by myself in the front of our house at Pant Cottage, and was standing close to the white retaining wall, which ran from the end of the house, down the length of the garden, and actually separated our garden from the rick-yard of Pant Farm, which was at a higher level than our garden, and I was looking toward the farm, when I felt something on my shoe, looking down I was horrified to see a long snake, slowly slide over my foot, and disappear into a hole in the wall. I was transfixed and petrified as I watched it slide out of sight, whereupon I ran like a startled rabbit, down to the field where I knew Dad was working, where I suppose I babbled out a slightly exaggerated account of the aforementioned reptile.

I do have a terrible phobia of the horrible things to this day, and the mere sight of one even only on TV makes me ill.

I used to travel to school, by catching the school bus on the main road opposite the St Mellons County club, where I would wait with my two school friends, who lived in the cafe, situated opposite the club entrance, this café has long since closed down, but my friends names were, David and Peter Connolly.

We were soon on the move once again, when Dad obtained a job with a farmer, Mr Robert Parsons, who farmed Berry Hill Farm, Coedkernew, and we moved into our new home, "The Gardens", a thatched cottage, situated in a field, down off the main road near to the farm. I was still attending Bassaleg Grammar school, and my new school friend was a boy named, Raymond Hodgekiss, who lived in the attractive stone built house on the opposite side of the road to the farm.

We continued travelling on the school buses, and a craze started, as they sometime do, and in this instance, it was collecting the items which were known as match strikers, which were the chrome fittings to be found on the back of bus seats, used by smokers to light matches. It required a screw driver, to undo the two screws, holding these fittings in place, and very soon, every boy in our group had acquired the said implement, and the fittings were disappearing rapidly, as the fad grew, eventually the bus company launched an inquiry, and after a bit of elementary detection, the accusing fingers pointed at me and my friends.

One afternoon, I was "arrested" by a school Prefect, straight from the rugby pitch, where I had been playing for the school team in a game against St Julians school, and, still wearing my rugby kit, thin cotton shorts etc, I was ushered to the Headmaster's study, wondering frantically what on earth was so urgent. As I entered, I was subjected to a series of searching questions, and quickly realized that my friends had already been questioned, and "pleaded guilty as charged, ---me, "being of sound mind", soon realised that it would be futile to deny the charge.

I admitted everything to Mr Penry M. Rees, the headmaster, who was known to all, as "Blinkin" due to the way that he blinked frantically as he spoke, whereupon, he came straight to the point, and administered, my sentence, which was "Six of the best", across my nether-regions!!!, and I must admit, that I was blinking, rather more than him when he had finished !!

Our home, was as I have said earlier, a thatched cottage which was rather primitive, with a coal fire, no electricity or modern sanitation, the toilet was a chemical one, and was housed in the adjoining shed with a galvanised roof, which also was where we stored our coal and firewood, the water supply was a spring about twenty five yards away from the house and entailed carrying buckets full when we needed a bath, in order to fill the boiler which was just inside this shed, and on bath days to site the tin bath just inside the door, in broad daylight, as the lack of lighting made bath times a hit or miss affair,

Once the bath was in place, , the next task was to light the fire under the boiler, which was much easier said than done, one had to be both lucky and determined, as it entailed getting down on all fours, with ones face near to the fire aperture, and blowing to persuade the kindling wood to hopefully burst into flames, although from hours of experience, it hardly ever did, and it was quite usual to see one or more of us, looking like overworked chimney-sweeps, with eyes red and streaming, hands and knees, dirty and dusty. From our sessions at the fire hole, (or lack of fire!!,) hole, trying to persuade Mam that it might be more beneficial to have a quick wash with a damp flannel," for now" in the supposition that the wood would "definitely" burn better tomorrow !!!--by this time we were much dirtier than when we first started, but at least we now DID need a bath!!

It was at this time that Dad's health took a definite down turn, and lead to many bouts of hospital treatment over the ensuing years, and it was during one of these spells and his absence from the farm, that I decided to harness one of the shire-horses, or as we always called them, cart horses, and took it down the field and taught myself how to use a hay-sweep, not very successfully, I must add, but I had seen dad doing it, and it looked so easy then!!--but I must have been about twelve then.!!

Berry Hill Farm house was partly "let" to two old spinsters, named Waters, though we didn't see much of them, and in one of the lofts above the stables lived an old man named John Reekes, and the farm is actually situated off the left hand side of the main Newport to Cardiff road, just above the village of Coedkernew, it is now Berry Hill P.Y.O Farm, and before the M4 Motorway was constructed, this was a very busy road, and it was just outside our front gate that John Reekes was struck by a speeding car and fatally injured, this was the first time that we children had experience of death, the old man used candles to light his home, and I vividly remember that these candles and the carrier bags he had been carrying, were strewn along the road for many yards.

I had, by now, got an after school part time, job, on a bread round with dear old Ralph Ralls from the neighbouring village of Marshfield, who's father owned a shop and a bakery in that village, near the school. Ralph, was I guess, in his mid fifties, and drove a little grey van, I was paid one shilling per day after school, I kept threepence and gave Mam ninepence, and my job also entailed cleaning out a number of chicken houses, every Saturday, for which I received the princely sum of three shillings and sixpence.

Ralph was a tall, gaunt, man who rarely smiled, but if we were early arriving at our last customer, on a Friday evening in Commercial Road Newport, he would treat us to a cup of tea, and a bun. Mr Ralls would pick me up at 4.30 each afternoon and we would deliver to about eight houses, off Pencarn lane, near the new Duffryn estate, then we would deliver to the Gaer, Ridgeway, and finally end up at Commercial Road in Newport. Ralph had a habit of licking the lead of his pencil as he filled in the various deliveries we had completed, Our last call was at a news agents who I soon found to be a man named Mr Joe Carr, I had read about in my boxing magazines, he was a well known manager of professional boxers.

I used to spend all the time I could with Mr Carr, being very eager to get involved with the sport in any way I could, and over the ensuing years he proved to be a big help, he was noted for assisting young boxers from abroad and sponsoring them into the professional game in Britain.

Each Saturday I would go to Mr Ralph Ralls's house and clean out his numerous chicken houses, then I would go down the Marshfield road to the Bakery opposite the village school, and help to load the van for the afternoon deliveries, This was quite a pleasant task, in fact, I used to enjoy it because the fresh bread smelled terrific, and I used to receive freshly baked buns to eat, then we would go on the round delivering as usual.

Mr Edgar Ralls was a short, stocky man, with a bald head, and he wore spectacles, he was also a confirmed Methodist, Ralph was tall and gaunt looking, they are now buried in the family plot at the little graveyard, at the rear of what is now the Masonic Hall in Castleton.

It was from Berry Hill Farm that we started attending church at Michaelstone-y-Fedw, and would travel by bus to Castleton and then walk the long uphill journey to the church which is next door to the Cefn Mabley Arms. When we got off the bus Dad would quietly cut a long stick from the hedge and would usher us on the journey to church, he rarely had reason to use this stick, although we often did get a little unruly, but we KNEW when to stop.

My third sister Carol was born at Berry Hill, and was the baby of the family, Wendy and Peggy had arrived some years earlier, and we became Sunday school regulars at the little hall which is situated at the end of the crescent of what were, I believe, originally council houses in Coedkernew.

I said earlier that dad's health had deteriorated during our time here and it was one of his better spells that we moved into our next home, but also during our time at Berry Hill, I became close friends with my school mate, named Raymond Hodgekiss, who lived opposite Berry Hill farm, we used to travel to school together, and also joined the Boy Scout troop, the !st Bassaleg Troop. We also decided to build a "land yacht"--- this is a wooden triangular shaped base with a wheel on each corner, old pram wheels did the trick!, which had a tall mast fixed in the centre on which was hung a sail, made out of two old cotton bed sheets, the front wheel was on a swivel to enable us to steer the craft as we visualised it hurtling along in a strong wind.

We spent a lot of time scrounging the timber and materials, and our craft took shape in the pigsty, situated at the top of Raymond's father's garden, —we had nearly completed work on the building of our masterpiece, when unfortunately it became time for another move for the nomadic Bassett family.

I often pass by Raymond's old home, on my regular excursions to and from Castleton, it appears also to be a business premises now, we never did launch our craft, and I often wonder what happened to it, —the old pigsty is still visible from the road, I wonder is it still there..........

I used to like ice-cream ……!!

When we moved into Pant cottage at Tylla Lane, I enrolled at Bassaleg grammar school, and due to the fact that I had moved from various schools, in quick succession, from Abergavenny to Barry and now, Bassaleg, the application for free meals was an on going saga, as a result, on my first day at my new school, I was once again, given my required amount, of three shillings and six pence, and off I went to school, --this routine continued over the following weeks.

I enjoyed Bassaleg school, particularly the school dinners which were cooked on the premises, and much to my satisfaction there was always plenty of second helpings to be had, -- the "afters", such as steamed pudding, treacle tart, and many other varieties, were always in plentiful supply, and I used to take full advantage of this fact.....I was in "glutton heaven"!!

After lunch I would head straight for the main gates, where our old friend, "Knocker", the ice-cream man would be parked looking for trade, he sold such delights as, "Knockers specials", and "Tanner Cuts", though I would usually often have to forego these treats, due to lack of finance. Unlike today's youngsters, pocket money was unheard of in the Bassett household, , purely and simply due to lack of income, nevertheless I did have the pleasure of these delights often after fate, lent a hand, let me explain...

Dinner money was collected every Monday and I paid mine, until one Monday I was informed by the master, that clearance had been received for me to go onto the "Free Meal" list, leaving me with three and sixpence to burn a hole in my pocket, with an ice-cream van to provide an alternative, So anyway........I bought an ice-cream!...then another, ! And another!, ...until suddenly I discovered that all my dinner money had gone, --after much soul searching, I decided that no-one would be any the wiser, if I left it till next week to tell Mam that I would be GOING on the Free Meal list!.

The following Monday, I collected my dinner-money, and went off to school, and consequently, bought an ice-cream, and another, and so on, I was beginning to enjoy my new found source of income, but a small voice told me that I really SHOULD let Mam know, that I no longer had to pay for dinners, ...so I decided that this, is definitely the last week, ...the ice-creams certainly were delicious though.

One morning several weeks later, Mam received a letter, "To confirm that Robert William Melville Bassett, a pupil at the above school will continue to receive Free School Meals, until further notice "!!!------ -I assure you, dear reader, questions WERE asked, Admonition WAS carried out, swiftly and firmly, ...FULL STOP !!!

Good Bye, MR Rees.

While perusing the South Wales Argus, which I always enjoy reading, I was saddened to see that my old Head-Master, at Bassaleg Grammar School, the legendary Penry M. Rees had "passed away", at the grand old age, of ninety six years, I had telephoned him about three years ago, after reading a feature in the same local paper, where he had given a talk about the second World war, in which he had been a prisoner of war in a notorious Japanese prison camp, this talk had taken place at his adopted Victoria Road United Reform Church, and we had a pleasant chat about the old school, and he had chuckled when I reminded him that he had given me "Six of the best" in 1951.

The obituary notice, stated that his funeral service would take place at his old church and I went along to pay my respects to my old Head Master, in the hope that I might meet old colleagues, though I hadn't seen anyone from the old school since our reunion many years ago. I did see one old friend, a certain Doug Thomas, who was actually a year ahead of me in school but who had, in fact, returned to spend his entire adult career as a Teacher at the school, which in fact, had taken comprehensive status, he stayed until his eventual retirement.

It was a poignant afternoon, and I learned how Mr Rees had suffered terribly at the hands of the Japanese, and of the respect and high esteem in which he was held, by members of the United Reform Church, and I realized then, that this city had lost a well respected Gentleman.

I didn't attend the crematorium.

Mr Penry Markham Rees 1908—2005 R.I.P,

Chapter Five

Michaelstone-y-Fedw, "Thomas the mill", and work.

We moved into our new home at, No1 Bridge Terrace Michaelstone-y-Fedw, a village situated about six miles from Newport, consisting of a cluster of houses, about fifteen that is, a Post Office, and a Chapel, just over a mile away was the village school, a church, and a pub named The Cefn Mabley Arms, the school is now a residence for one of the new influx of moneyed people, who have taken over village life. We lived in one of a pair of semi-detached red brick houses, next door to another large family of eight children, so with my three brothers and three sisters, there always seemed to be lots of activity going on.

I was still attending Bassaleg Grammar school, and each day I would cycle up to the vicarage to call for my pal, Peter Jones-Evans, the vicars younger son, —though to call our machines bicycles, is a bit of an exaggeration, because though my bike was reasonable, I had fixed a front mudguard over the rear wheel to prevent water soaking my back on wet days, but Peter's, or as he was known, PJ's, machine, had only one pedal, and no brakes, he seemed to gain some advantage from bringing it rattling and squeaking from his father's garage. And my bike had a tendency to miss the cogs when I pedalled so that very often I would be frantically pedalling and not moving!!.

PJ was built like a tank, and was always ready for a bit of rough and tumble, -- half way to the bus rout at Castleton, we would meet our "enemy" from Penylan, Donald Western, who was a pupil at the "posh" Clarke's College, in Cardiff, and from then on, for the rest of the journey, it would be a succession of wrestling, and ramming each other into the hedges on the roadside, and by the time we reached Castleton, it was obvious that we hadn't walked in orderly fashion, far from it, PJ made "Just William", look like a fashion icon!!, --I should perhaps point out that Donald Western wasn't our enemy really, it was just boyish larking about, – we would have the "return match" on the journey home.

It was also at this time that I started doing a "paper round", in an effort to earn some pocket money, I collected the papers from the little shop opposite the Marshfield road junction, in Castleton and proceeded to deliver them on my homeward journey, —I only delivered about thirty or so, which earned me about two shillings per week, but of course I had given up my job on the bread round with Mr Ralls so finances were at an all time low!!

I then became friendly with Mr Thomas who farmed the little Mill Farm, close to our new home in Michaelstone consisting of about forty acres which I reached by going down the long lane near our house. I had discovered that he owned a Ferguson tractor, and after a couple of visits I persuaded him to "let me have a go" on it, and quite soon I became quite adept at the various jobs, such as ploughing harrowing and mowing, which arguably are among the prime jobs with a tractor.

Ferguson Tractors were the innovators of a completely new hydraulic lifting system, which allowed the implements to be raised and lowered at the touch of a small lever, with the result that jobs which used to take years to master, using horses, the mainstay of farming, now became much easier to do, even so, it still took a certain amount of natural ability to handle the modern technology of tractors, and the implements available.

Most evenings and weekends, would see me busy in the fields at the rear of our new home, on the Fergie' until often quite late at night, working by the light of the tractor headlights, even though I was still only just gone thirteen years of age, the reader may no doubt, be wondering when I, a grammar school pupil, found the time to complete my homework, usual among the high schools, the fact is, I would then be "beavering away" right up to lesson time, in the morning after, in a usually futile attempt to have it ready for collection---------I wasn't an ideal pupil !!

Although I used to work a lot of hours at Mill Farm, I rarely seemed to get paid, and often I would pluck up the courage to ask Mr Thomas for some pay.--- Mr Thomas, whose name was Mervyn, was a pleasant little man, and had rather a "battle axe" of a wife named, "Helen", and one small son named "Peter", and without being unkind I would say that as farmers go, Mr Thomas was not the greatest, but he was happy to scrape a living on his pleasant little farm.

On one occasion I had plucked up the courage to ask him for some pay, he told me to let him have a list of what he owed me, I was elated, and during the following day I wrote out a list of start and finish times, and a "bill", which came to about two pounds ten shillings, £2.50 in decimal money, which I presented to him the following day, Mr Thomas then asked me, would I like a glass of home brewed cider?, I said yes, whereon he gave me a large glass, and told me to fill it from the barrel in the dairy, which I duly did, and drank it, he then asked me would I like another, which I drank, and another...............I cant remember what happened about my wage demand !!! but I do recall that I had tremendous problems with my bike, negotiating the dark lane on my homeward journey, and to make matters worse, I got a puncture in the front wheel, as a result of riding into a clump of blackthorn bushes in the dark lane, I fell off, ... and by the time I had found my way to our house, I was looking very bedraggled and covered in scratches and grazes.

On another occasion when I approached him again for some pay, he invited me to try on a suit of clothes for size, now at the age of fourteen I was tall and rather skinny, I remember Mam telling someone "that I had outgrown my strength", and although I had no idea what on earth that meant, I wallowed in self pity for ages afterwards!!!--anyway I tried the suit on and it"sort of" fitted me, so he told me to keep it, and I took it home, feeling rather pleased as I had never owned a suit before.

I wore my "new suit" to the end of year, form Christmas Party at school, and felt great, --in hindsight, I must have looked ridiculous, because it was royal blue in colour with thin red stripes, the trousers were very wide at the bottom, and the jacket had wide lapels, OH!! and I wore a silk tie belonging to elder brother Arthur, --the one with a woman in a bathing costume on, --I MUST have looked like a youthful "Arfur Daley", I wonder why I never "pulled" that year either!!

The Morgan family who lived next door, were an unusual bunch, and consisted of father, George, mother, Maud, sons, Walter, Billy, David, Arthur, and Frank, daughters, Margaret, Phyllis and Janet and without being too unkind, they were not the brightest of families, but they did have some unique customs at mealtimes, each had their own rations of butter, sugar, tea, bread and individual pots of jam, which certainly filled the huge table in the centre of the living room, but, despite this strange arrangement it seemed to work for them, each knew their tasks in the running of the home and there were never any arguments or disputes and the house was spotless.

The Morgan family while not likely to amaze folk with their intellect, they were always clean and tidy, and were always willing to work, and did, —they never argued or caused any problems, in fact I only wish that there were more families like them, around today.

As I have already said, most of my spare time was spent at Mill Farm, but occasionally brother Noel and I would spend time outside the house, playing football on the lane outside our front gate, with whatever ball we could find, I always insisted on playing down the slope, as I was the elder brother, and HE would have the task of chasing the ball, after I had scored as there was a steep fall in the road just past our houses......
Noel would go galloping after it as it gathered speed down the hill.!!!

Over the years, I have finished this "book" and often given copies to various family members, having since then, continued expanding the stories and recalling more anecdotes and events, and hopefully the reader will now appreciate that I am converting this manuscript into chapters, but there will be times when this "plan will be put on hold ", in order to include an added event or story of interest.

At Michaelstone we lived in the first of a pair of semi-detached houses, the gardens joined onto another four blocks of semis, which were fronted by what can be best described, as a "green", with a cul-de-sac road running the length of the fronts. In the first of these houses live a certain Jack and Connie Adams, and their little son, Kenneth, The wife's brother Arthur's mate, Victor Davidge, lodged with them. Vic was a tidy lad and worked at a neighbouring farm, owned by Bill Jones, the farm was called Bridge Farm.

Arthur, and Vic were good friends, being roughly the same age, and Vic who owned a gleaming maroon Rudge Whitworth bicycle, would pay me two shillings and sixpence, at regular intervals to ride this machine to the bike shop on Cardiff Road, Newport, owned by Geoff Prosser, for it to be serviced, I would do this by riding it to Bassaleg Grammar school, then afterwards I would cycle down Forge Lane and into Newport to the shop, I would then catch the bus home which used to travel through the village a couple of times each day, on its way to and from Cardiff to Newport. I would then receive a similar fee to go and collect it when ready, a day or so later.

While we were at this address, Brother David, obtained a job at a small market gardens owned by, an American ex Army Colonel, name Barring -Gould, and later had me taken on as his part time assistant, I enjoyed working there apart from the fact that David would "wind me up" unmercifully, on occasions. Some of the work was tedious, such as sifting compost, for hours on end, but I did enjoy the planting using a marked rod which the Colonel had devised which marked where to put each plant, so that no matter which way you looked at the gardens, the plants ALWAYS appeared in straight rows.

I was, what Dad called, "heavy handed", and we often had to water the long cold frames using a hose and spray, this job took ages and we would draw the glass frame covers back and sit "lightly" on the glass, at first, but unfortunately I would often relax a little too much and consequently the pane of glass would suddenly shatter and I would fall through. These were the things David would tease me about, and he had been "ribbing" me for some time, this particular day, when I lost my temper, and grabbed a garden fork, and chased after him, David was very fast on his feet and after chasing him vainly in and out of the greenhouses, in sheer frustration I hurled the garden fork, like a javelin, ---it hit David and stuck in his leg---It frightened the life out of me, and David limped for ages afterwards.

The Colonel also kept a lot of honey bees, and during warm weather they would be very "active" and would often pitch on our heads and hands, I hated the things and one hot day, the Colonel, after watching me tearing up and down the gardens, arms flailing wildly at these confounded bees, called out to me to "get the Hell outer here, you're fired!!!"

The Colonel thought the world of David though, he always called him "Sydeney", and I can still "hear" him saying "Put a bit of slug killer "orn the latterses, Sydeney" in his strong American drawl. Each Saturday he would take David in his fully loaded large American estate car to the Newport Indoor market to work on the stall selling plants and produce, while I stayed home sifting compost. We did also enjoy our tea breaks of plates of toast and hot tea in the greenhouses, I still recall the lovely aromas in the glass-houses.

As I have mentioned earlier, this manuscript has been updated and enlarged a number of times, and I have since been back to this place which was named "Colscote Gardens", but it has been extensively altered and is now a trout farm, where the glasshouses once stood, are now large breeding fish tanks and it has been landscaped, but it doesn't please the eye, as the plants once did, when they were symmetrically planted using the old Colonel's special marking rods............

Hooray, We Are Mobile!!!.

In the 50's or thereabouts, my eldest brother Arthur, who had been working for Cambrian United Dairies, at their Marshfield Depot, announced to a startled Bassett household that he was buying a car, from one of the Dairy drivers, a certain Roy Taylor, affectionately known as "Dropper", for reasons we never discovered !!.

The news certainly caused more than a few few ripples of interest in both the Bassett and the Morgan family, who lived next door, at 1 and 2 Bridge Terrace Michaelstone-y-Fedw, in fact they too, were contemplating buying a car also, as it later transpired. During the ensuing days and weeks as Arthur negotiated the purchase of the aforementioned vehicle, he fuelled our interest, with descriptions of "THE CAR", "which is a Morris Cowley, and has large chrome headlamps, a gleaming chrome radiator and had also been newly painted, and goes like a bomb!!"------his words not mine!.

The big day arrived, and Arthur arrived home in it!!!...........Our car was, as I recall, exactly as described, newly hand painted blue and black, with huge chrome headlights and radiator, and I can vividly remember, spending many hours, with Arthur tinkering with the engine, with me sat inside, with him yelling "press the pedal!" or, "try it now"!, until sometimes it would burst into life--------rather like a demented sewing machine, with me pressing and depressing the pedals as fast as I could..........then it would "phut, phut, phut!!" and stop.!!

It was all good fun though, the car had rather a unique pedal formation, unlike modern cars in that the accelerator pedal was at the front between the clutch and the brake pedals, with the result that one had to be something of an acrobat to move ones feet, in order to operate these pedals, and keep the engine running.

One other unfortunate discovery I was unlucky enough to make, was, that someone had accidentally spilled acid on the rear seat, which incidentally was a large piece of foam rubber, and over the ensuing weeks, my grey school-trousers, gradually disintegrated and were ruined. The acid had apparently leaked from a car battery which had been placed on the seat sometime earlier..

Our car certainly had a lot of chrome, the lights and the radiator were highly polished, but, I cant recall the car ever doing many miles in use, in fact, I do remember the hedge of Dad's garden was removed, and the vehicle seemed to know that it had arrived HOME, as it settled to rest in the corner of the garden!!.

For the life of me, I cannot remember what eventually became of it, The Morgan family actually bought a Ford 10, which compared to our CAR, was a black "ugly brute", but I don't think theirs lasted long either !!!.

Chapter Six

My First Job, The Boss, Ty-Hir Farm

At the age of fifteen I left school at the second attempt, ---- let me explain, my birthday falls in October, and I, being eager to leave and start work, decided in my infinite wisdom, that I would leave at the beginning of the summer holidays, in July of that year. It seemed sensible to me, so in the days leading up to the summer break, I handed in all of my text books, and said my goodbyes to all of my class mates etc, even to the point of receiving good luck handshakes from the teaching fraternity at Bassaleg Grammar school, and I "Left" and started work at Pendlebury's Fairwater farm, in the village, and all was well, until about the second week of the September, the same year, when Mam received a letter questioning my whereabouts from the school.

Several days later, a man from the Education Department came to the house, and informed us that I had no right leaving, when I was after all, only fourteen, he explained that the ruling was, that pupils were allowed to leave at "the end of the term in which one obtained the school leaving age of fifteen" and that I MUST attend school immediately, FULL STOP!!! Failure to do so would entail a summons. The next day, I went to school, much to the amusement of the pupils and staff, and I spent some time explaining the whys and wherefores, of my reappearance at school, only now I was in Form V, having left school in IV North, I continued at school till the start of the Christmas Holidays when the school "broke up" again------I left, for the second time..........

When I resumed my career at Pendlebury's Dad and David, were already working there, Mam and I had been working part time previously for some months, our jobs included simple manual work, such as hoeing, packing cabbages to be despatched to retail outlets in the towns etc, but because Mr Bernard Pendlebury was aware that I could drive a tractor, from my time at Mill farm, I soon got the chance to do simple tractor work, at my new place of work, such as, working with Bill Morgan, our next door neighbours son, doing a job called steerage hoeing, which entailed me driving the tractor, very slowly up and down the rows of plants as Bill sat on the machine behind to guide it, as it removed the weeds from around the said plants.

This soon became very tedious, for hour after hour, --- Bill wasn't the most genial of characters, being slow witted and somewhat dull, but it was better than being in the labouring gang doing the manual hoeing etc, and working at Pendlebury's wasn't too bad, in fact it was quite enjoyable, but one evening whilst reading the local "South Wales Argus", I noticed an advert, which said that "a young man" was required at "Ty Hir Farm", which is actually opposite Fairwater Farm, but is a Dairy Farm as opposed to a market garden, being primarily a milk producing and grassland farm, the type that Dad and all the family had always been involved in.

The advert contained a telephone number, and without further ado, I borrowed some change off Mam, and went over the phone box and called the number, and spoke to a man, who said that it was"D.R Wyatt speaking!", and after a short conversation, I was invited to go and see him at the farm, so I had a quick wash, and rode my bike to the farm, and met the person who was to have a big influence on me, over the years ahead, ---Mr David Wyatt, and although many years later he actually "fired" me, I have always admired and tried to model myself on the man I remember, even though many years passed before I managed to resume my friendship with those lovely people.

Ty Hir Farm is situated on the road from Michaelstone toward Cefn

Mably Hospital, which was I believe, an isolation hospital for tuberculosis sufferers, many years ago, but I dont think it is in use now, I think that a farm for rare breeds, now occupies the site, with the building as a visitors centre or such like, After speaking to Mr Wyatt, I was given the job, as advertised, working on a dairy farm as a general farm worker, and I met the present incumbent of the job I had acquired, his name was Ray Clements, who was leaving to take up his own farm at Carrow Hill near Chepstow, but who, as a favour for his friend, Mr Wyatt, was staying on for an extra fortnight or so to "show me the ropes", such as the use of electric fences etc, and the general jobs around the farm.

I soon realised that Ray was a terrific chap, and also a very conscientious worker too, and that he would be a hard act to follow, he had also lived with the Wyatts during his time at Ty Hir, but Mr Wyatt was a very personable and likeable man, and I soon settled into the job.

Mr Wyatt, which was always how I addressed him, in those days, was a tall, slim man, handsome, with jet black hair, moustache, gleaming white, even teeth, and obviously very fit too, energetic and fastidious, in that everything had to be done correctly and efficiently, for example, cattle need to be milked at regular intervals, eg twice daily at twelve hour intervals and so on, for maximum productivity, and that is what he aimed for. Mrs Wyatt, was also a very striking woman, being fair haired, and very attractive too, and to a young pimply youth like me, an unobtainable goddess, they made a perfect couple.

The Wyatt's had two small children at that time, Martin, the eldest was about three years old, and his little brother Steven, some two years younger, like their parents Martin had black hair and Steven had fair hair, they often used to play together, in the farm yard, particularly in the sand pile which was on the concrete, outside the cow shed, it was a pleasure to hear them playing.

Mr Wyatt never used swear words, but when perhaps he was in the occasional, bad mood, he would say things like, "for crying out loud", or "stars!", or "the thundering things", but what did sound very comical, was to hear little Martin or Steven, say those same things, when or if, one of them got a bit frustrated with one of their toys or games.

The Ty Hir herd, consisted of mainly Friesian cattle, with about ten Jersey animals to improve the quality of the milk, or butterfat content, there was also a pedigree Jersey bull, and it was this animal which was to cause me many embarrassing moments, let me explain, I was at that time, just turned fifteen years old, and as they say, quite naïve about the "facts of life" and at certain times, the cows would be "ready" for a "visit" from the aforementioned bull.

When it was time for one of the cows to "enjoy" the company of the bull, I would then be required to hold the cow with a halter, and Mr Wyatt would bring the bull with a pole attached to the ring in its nose, and he would then encourage the bull to "do the necessary", and often Mrs Wyatt would casually lean on the yard gate, to watch or assist if needed, I was at that time, a shy teenager, and I used to get pretty embarrassed, and "hot under the collar", but looking back, I guess it was rather funny, and I did learn about the "cows and the bull", if not exactly about the "birds and the bees".

I really enjoyed working at Ty Hir, and I learned many things, under the fatherly guidance of Mr Wyatt, but occasionally I would make mistakes in the process, some more serious than others, and even now, thinking back I can remember some of them. One being, when I forgot to shut the hatch on the chicken house, one evening, with the result, that in the morning, we discovered all the hens scattered around the orchard with their heads bitten off, by marauding foxes during the night, these poultry were the personal property of the Wyatt family, but although I obviously deserved a "rollicking", I distinctly remember that though he must have been "fuming", Mr Wyatt hardly raised his voice to me.

On another day, I had been working on the silage pit, during the day, spreading new mown grass, Mr Wyatt asked me had I seen any money anywhere, ? I answered truthfully that I had not, and it transpired that a roll of white(and black) five pound notes had been dropped by the owner of Ty Hir Farm, a certain J Roy Paton, who was visiting the place that day, and they had been lying feet away from where I had been labouring all afternoon. The fact was, I had never seen a five pound note in my life!!!

Mr Paton, was a wealthy business man, who lived in the neighbouring village of Lisvane, near Cardiff, and was the Managing Director of a large engineering company who manufactured mining equipment, and I guess that the farm was a tax saving project for him. Mr Wyatt was the Farm Bailiff, my boss.--- Mr Paton was also the Master of the Llangibby Fox Hounds, and as such had a number of horses stabled at our farm, one of these was an old Chestnut horse named"Tex", and another, a former race horse, named "Cottage Bud", which I believe was a descendant of the Grand National winner, "Sheilla's Cottage", Mrs Wyatt, who loved animals, would go riding as often as she could around the village, and also around the fields at Ty Hir farm, and although there isn't any bus service through the village now, it was, even in those far off days, a lovely quiet area.

When Mr Paton, came in his cream and gold Bentley car, on his regular visits, to walk around the farm, he always had his trusty "thumb-stick", and usually at the end of his walk, he would put his foot on the edge of the water tank, and I would have the privilege of washing his "wellies", whilst he was still wearing them. Mr Wyatt would often take me on the tractor and trailer to Mr Patons large house in Lisvane and we would spend the day cultivating or tidying the large walled garden, usually during a warm summer day.....I enjoyed this break from the farm, although we would of course, have to give the cattle their evening "milking", and feed the calves etc.........but this wasn't really classed as work, it was just something which was part of the daily routine.

Mrs Wyatt's step sister, a girl named Jane Padfield, who was at that time about twelve, and lived in Cross Keys, would come to Ty Hir to stay for the week ends and school holidays, and I developed quite a "crush" on her, and it made my day, to hear the Land-Rover arrive back, during evening milking, on a Friday, and to catch sight of her as they got out, but I would be really depressed if, for any reason, she hadn't come.

Each morning after milking, Mr Wyatt, who had started work at about six am, before I had arrived at eight am, would go to the house, to have his breakfast, and Mrs Wyatt would bring me an aluminium milk jug full of tea and a plate of hot toast, which I would enjoy eating in the dairy, for my "elevenses", and again in the evening, before we started milking, Mr Wyatt, would go in for his tea, as I brought the cows in, he would then bring back the jug of tea, and a plate of cucumber, and salad cream sandwiches, when he came back out, which I would eat ravenously, because, in those days I was always ready and eager to eat, and I did enjoy these simple treats.

One Christmas, the Wyatt's gave me a "Smiths" pocket watch, and showed me how to safeguard it, by keeping it in a polish tin padded with cotton wool, --- these tins had a butterfly opener on the side, and I was absolutely "thrilled to bits", to be the proud possessor of a real pocket watch, exactly like my"Boss".

Ty Hir Farm was a modern, forward looking establishment in those days, and we were one of the innovators of strip grazing fields, by using electric fencing, we also had facilities and the machinery for drying grass, and when we used it, the results were terrific, in fact I would have happily eaten the dried grass myself, it smelled so appetizing, we were also one of the first places in Wales to make silage, this being the early fifties, remember. We also weighed and recorded the individual milk yield of each cow, at every milking, and I used to enjoy taking the weekly record sheets home to total up every individual sheet, ready for the visit of the official recorder, who was employed by the Milk Marketing Board, a certain Mr Roberts, who would come and take samples and other details of the herd, which were then taken to the main Offices of the MMB. He would call about every six weeks or so. Mr Wyatt did receive an award for "The Best Small Herd" from the "Farmers Weekly", the trade magazine, in the early fifties.

The first year I was at Ty Hir, Mr Wyatt had a big new silage pit built, adjoining the yard at the end of the cow-sheds, and this entailed removing a lot of soil from the orchard behind, and removing the high retaining wall and digging a huge hole back into the orchard, to accommodate the space required for the pit, walls were then built to about eight feet in height, and a huge Nissan type hut, was used to form a roof over the whole construction, the floor was then concreted, and drainage installed, this was required because silage actually gives off a lot of liquid, as the grass etc is compounded to prevent it heating up, the secret of good silage is keeping the product at the correct temperature to allow it to mature---the cattle loved it and as a result our milk output increased too.

During the days when this new innovation was emptied and the time it would then be re-filled it could be used as storage, and in fact, I have been back to the old place quite recently and it is now used for that purpose all the time, double doors have also been added for security.

During the harvest when the pit required filling, I would arrive in work at eight o'clock each morning, the Boss would be half way through the morning milking, and we would complete this task, he would go for his, well earned breakfast, while I then fed the calves etc, and cleaned the cowsheds, and washed the dairy utensils, Mrs Wyatt would bring me out a jug of tea and rounds of toast, as mentioned earlier. The routine jobs finished I would report to the house, for my orders and often at this time, it would be for me to take the Ferguson TVO tractor, fitted with a hydraulic mower, and mow a part of the field of grass, Mr Wyatt would then spend an hour or so, driving the heavy standard Fordson tractor, back and forth on the newly cut and layered grass of the previous days toil, to compress it prior to another layer being added, Wilted grass soon heats up and spoils if it isn't compressed which is why silage needs to be rolled a lot during the filling of the pit.

A year or so later, we were joined by a man named Tony Edwards, who lived in Draethen a neighbouring village towards Caerphilly, or as he was known locally as "Big Sam", being a heavily built fellow, who facially, looked a lot like the American film star, Robert Mitchum, and during that years silage, making I drove the TVO Fergie', and Tony drove the newly acquired diesel Ferguson as we hurtled to and from the various fields, hauling the newly cut grass which Mr Wyatt levelled and spread, in the pit. To carry the grass we had what were known as "Buck Rakes" fitted to the rear of the tractors which were hydraulically operated to raise or lower the implements –Grass is heavy and when the buck rakes were raised loaded on the rear of the tractors the weight on the back would cause the front wheels to lift off the floor, and Tony and I would hang on for dear life as we hurtled to and fro, with the front wheels lifting, which made the tractors look like two berserk grass hoppers bouncing along ahead of a cloud of dust from the rear wheels. !!

Being young, I discovered after some time, that I actually was missing the banter of the crowd of people, that used to work at Pendlebury's during the summer months, such as all the "townies" who would arrive from Maesglas, Newport, and Llanrumney near Cardiff, for casual work in the fields, and I foolishly decided to go back to Pendlebury's and did so, but then after a short while I began to miss the one on one work and relationship I had at Wyatt's at Ty Hir Farm, so I then asked Mr Wyatt if I could go back and work at Ty Hir, and thankfully he allowed me to return, and I was so relieved to go back.

It was actually, I think, more enjoyable with the company of Tony Edwards, and we built up a good working relationship and when Mr Wyatt wanted to go to market, or where-ever, we were good company for each other, and me being boxing mad, we would often have light hearted sparring sessions, out of sight of the Boss, Tony was an amiable even tempered person, about twelve year older than I, and I used to enjoy larking about, with him, he was a tidy man, and a number of times he invited me to accompany him, to Worcestershire in his little van, to visit his relatives, which I enjoyed very much, during summer evenings.

Ty Hir Farm house, was rather a large long building, and was rather a foreboding place on dark winter evenings, with only a small cottage, close by as a neighbour, and in the early fifties, we hadn't yet had the luxury of Television in our house, so when Mr Wyatt asked me to sit with Mrs Wyatt some evenings when he had to go out, I agreed readily, because they had TV even though it was only a nine inch screen, I loved watching the programmes, but when the time to go home came, in the night, I found that the pictures played havoc with my eyesight, I had awful difficulties, negotiating the dark lanes around Michaelstone on my homeward journey, --- even so those were lovely times and such a pleasure to look back on.

One day in early 1958, we were given the shocking news that the farm was going to be sold by Auction, lock, stock and barrel, Mr Wyatt was leaving, --- at that time, I had no idea where the family were going, or why, but, rightly or wrongly I believe to this day, that it was Mr Wyatt's leaving that prompted Mr Paton to sell up and retire, I learned later that the Wyatt family had taken over a small farm on the well known Curre Estate, near Chepstow, and that their home would be just outside the small market town of Usk, situated in between Usk and Chepstow. I don't think Mr Paton relished the thought of trying to find a man to replace our "Boss".

As I have stated earlier, Ty Hir was a modern thinking established farm, and one implement we had then, was a hedge-cutter, which was mounted behind the drivers seat on the tractor, and consisted of a long central mounted tubular arm, with a large six foot long blade, powered by a large petrol engine mounted on the other end, this arm could be turned through three hundred and sixty degrees, the cutter could be set at different angles and required the tractor to be driven by myself slowly at a walking pace, while the operator, Mr Wyatt, guided the cutter along the hedge. While I type it has occurred to me that this machine must have placed a heck of a lot of strain on the neck and shoulder muscles of the operator, but at the time I never gave it a thought.

I am still very interested in old farm practices and machinery, such as David Brown and Ferguson tractors, and I have bought many videos of farming, and on one is a farmer using what was known as a "fiddle" to sow grass seeds, which required the operator to march at a regular pace to and fro across the field, while using the fiddle part to spread the seeds uniformly and this brings back memories of Mr Wyatt doing just that when he sowed the grass in the ten acre field at Ty Hir about fifty five years ago.....Happy Days.!!

Another thing that the Boss was good at, and obviously enjoyed, was building work, and whilst we were at Ty Hir he built a superb drive on milk stand, at the main gate, and later refurbished two cow sheds with modern fittings and floors, he seemed capable of doing many jobs, AND making first class jobs of them too.

Over the years since my enforced retirement through ill health, I enjoy sitting and reminiscing and this has led me to increasing and enlarging this manuscript, as something or other, comes flooding back, -- as I write, I have just remembered a time when Mr and Mrs Wyatt went away for the day and left me on my own to do what ever job I had been given, after I had done the routine work, unbeknown to me they had left the Alsatian dog in the house. During the day I had been busy, but around mid afternoon, a violent thunder-storm had scared me, -- when the time came, I brought the cows in and got things ready for the Boss to do the milking later that afternoon..-- It had been thundering quite a bit through the day, which worried me, as I did not like lightening one bit, but it had passed, and I was busy getting things ready, when I casually glanced toward the house, ...and almost fell over with the shock of what I saw, !!! the kitchen window of the house had completely GONE, !!! I could not believe my eyes, !! I ran across and stared into the gaping hole where the window had been, ...It was a chaotic shambles inside.

For some time I stared in disbelief, then panic set in, and I thought, what am I going to tell the Wyatt's when they return home, I bet they'll think I did it!! cos I've been the only one here all, or most of the day--

--and that blinkin' thunder almost scared me to death, and now this!!, I worried myself silly for what seemed like ages, and then I heard the unmistakable sounds of the Land Rover coming up the drive..........I need not have worried, as it turned out that "Foreman" the poor Alsatian dog had been equally frightened of the storm earlier, and had literally torn the window out, in order to escape from the empty house.----------I wonder if Mr and Mrs Wyatt remember that little episode?

Chapter Seven

Enter Mr Kelly, and "those flaming sheep"

The Auction at Ty Hir Farm, was I believe a successful day, for Mr Paton, though I don't think the prices for the livestock were as good as was expected, but Mr Wyatt was happy because he actually successfully bid for a lot of the animals he had reared himself in his sojourn at the farm, he also bought farm implements to take with him to his own farm, and eventually all the stock and equipment was removed by the buyers, at the time I was happy in the knowledge that I had been "taken on" by the new owner of the farm, I was extremely pleased when Mr Wyatt told me that my job was safe at Ty Hir, but I soon came to realise that I would not be so contented--- as the days passed.

My new boss was a man named Mr Donald Kelly, an accountant in Ireland, who was closing his business and returning to Wales to take up agriculture, and would be taking up residence in seven or eight weeks time. His father, Mr Fred Kelly and his Uncle Mr Bill Kelly farmed the neighbouring Church Farm near the Cefn Mably Arms, and St Michaels Church in the village, and Mr Fred Kelly began to make sporadic visits to Ty Hir, these began to get more regular as the days passed, then a small flock of about fifty sheep were delivered by two stock lorries, and were put in the appropriately named Bank field, where-upon they promptly decided that "they" preferred the surrounding fields and just walked straight through the hedges which previously had been perfectly good enough for cattle, but sheep would go through even the smallest of gaps under a tidy hedge, and it became painfully obvious that these perishing animals would need very careful attention over the coming weeks., to prevent them from going "walkabout" if or when the mood struck them!!

After the Auction, and all the ensuing activity, the comings and goings had stopped, the farm became a quiet and somewhat sad place, the house was deserted, and of course there were no dogs, because the Wyatt's two, "Peter", the little black and white rough haired terrier, and "Foreman", the big Alsatian, were conspicuous by their absence, in the past, anyone approaching the house, were greeted by them barking shrilly.

After about three or four weeks, this changed, when a farmer from, New House Farm at St Brides Wentloog, a Mr Johnny Wintour, who apparently had bought the "standing" field of Kale, and the full pit of new silage, which we had made earlier in the year, --- came to have use of the milking facilities during the approaching winter months, in order to use all the aforementioned fodder . The arrival of the stock and equipment belonging to Mr Wintour, also heralded the the return to Ty Hir Farm, of my old mate Tony Edwards, if only temporary as he had obtained employment with that farmer, and would be taking care of their stock.

So apart from the house being empty, and the Wyatt family having departed for "pastures new", for me and "Sam" it was rather a case of"deja vu", --- Tony and I worked unsupervised at the farm for some months, I for my new employer, and Tony for Mr Wintour, he was doing a "sound job" too, Single-handedly milking the herd, looking after the additional young stock, each day he would load a huge load of freshly cut silage from the pit, and disappear to their farm at St Brides, later in the day he would arrive back to carry out the evening milking.

My flagging interest was roused one day, when a brand new "Ferguson 35", tractor and several implements to go with it arrived, this did rouse my interest, because it was the very latest model and the first of its kind in our area. But then early in the new year Mr Wintour and Tony, began to remove their stock and equipment, which was a surprise, but it transpired that the Kelly's had "gone back" on the sales agreement, with Mr Wintour, and insisted that they vacated the premises forthwith. I never heard what exactly happened, it seemed very strange, but my new Boss, Mr Donald Kelly soon showed his true colours on a number of occasions, as I was soon to realise, myself.

My new employer and his family arrived shortly afterwards, consisting of his wife and two children, Mr Donald Kelly was a tall youngish looking, bony faced man, with fair wispy hair, and wore spectacles, his wife was youngish, slim, and looked rather like his sister, and it was amazing how alike they were!. After some weeks things began to settle and take on a style of farming which came as no surprise to me, a number of pedigree cows were purchased and the cowshed was soon filled with animals which made it pretty obvious that my new boss was definitely not short of money, as a steady influx of pedigree animals arrived following his visits to stock sales around the Principality, and in all fairness to the man, he was making a fair job of getting into farming.

Even though Mr Kelly was doing a fair job of running his farm, he was a difficult person to take to, or his family, because unlike his father Mr Fred Kelly or, his uncle Mr Bill Kelly, who were affable old gentlemen, Donald was a typical educated "Twit", and many things about him, and his family began to irritate me, Donald had the habit of calling people, "stupid porpoises", and these sayings were often repeated by his son, Martin, which was accompanied by a leering smirk. Mr Kelly always had his family "in tow" if or when he came out to see, or talk to me, where-ever I might be working, and things came to a head one warm day.

I had been been ploughing a field near to the farm house, and they arrived "in force", one afternoon when I had been having rather a frustrating time, trying all ways to get the plough to dig to the required depth, in what was a difficult stony piece of ground, which had never been ploughed before, and had by this time been joined by Donald and his wife, and their two off-spring, walking along, back and forth across the field, as I wrestled with the controls and adjustments on the machine, getting intermittent shouts and advice, from the various members of his entourage, such as"try this" or "lower that", and other things or whatever they could think of, until I could"take" no more, so I stopped the tractor, climbed down from the drivers seat, and walked away in the direction of the farm yard.

Mr Kelly called out to me, to ask what I was doing, where-upon I turned and told them to decide who was going to drive the tractor, because, "I'm going home, Good Day"!!

The next day, I received a message from Mrs Kelly, -- Donald's mother, who lived at Church Farm, asking me to call in and see them, which I did, and was offered extra wages if I would go back to work for Donald, I knew that it would be a waste of time, but as I had no other plans, I agreed, and returned to Ty Hir and Mr Kelly.--- I had, in the meanwhile, been visiting the Wyatt's at their new farm at Llangwm on weekends, and this fact probably made the Kelly family even more unpleasant, by comparison, it was a surprise invitation from Mr Wyatt to go and "live in" and work at Coed-y-Ferm Farm for him, which gave me the alternative I had been seeking, and consequently I gave notice to Mr Kelly, and left Ty Hir Farm for good, as far as work was concerned.

I never saw, or spoke to the Kelly family again, but I don't think they lasted very long at Ty Hir Farm, and I believe Mr Donald Kelly died shortly afterwards. The current owners of Ty Hir and it seems, --- practically all the land from the vicarage down to the river bridge in Michaelstone village ----is a family named Richards, I have been to Ty Hir Farm on a number of occasions, to hog roasts and on two private visits and the farm doesn't seem to be an active farm, all the fields are tidy and grassed but appear to require a bit of TLC, as the grass is old and there doesn't seem to be much "going on" as a business. I also visited Mill Farm and discovered that the buildings had been converted into smart living accommodation, the old farm house was in use, and a large new bungalow had been built half way down the lane to the farm, which I believe is home for Mr Richards' mother.

Pendlebury's, Fairwater Farm is no longer a farm, the property has been bought by Peter Thomas, a multi millionaire, NOT the son of "Thomas, the Mill", rather the owner of "Peter's Savoury Products", well known pork pie manufacturers, Mr Fred Kelly's Church Farm is also owned by the Richard's of Ty Hir, although the old farm buildings have long since gone or purchased by the owners of the Cefn Mably Arms Inn.--- Colscot Gardens, Colonel Barring Gould's old place has been landscaped and turned into a trout farm, with numerous fish stock tanks, where the greenhouses were once sited. And I recently spotted a planning application to turn Pendlebury's Fairwater Farm, into yet another golf course.

I have on many occasions visited the Cefn Mably Arms, with my wife Jeannette, and often sister Margarette, husband Alan and brother David for lunch, and at the same time visited the Church which is open and discovered that Donald Kelly died in 1971, thirteen years after he bought Ty Hir, at the early age of 49 years old, his father Fred and his Uncle William both died in 1967, and his mother two years earlier in 1965, and are all buried in the churchyard.

As I write, today July 11th 2006, finds me eagerly looking forward to what I think will be another pleasant and hopefully an enjoyable return to the old farm, when Jeannette and I along with Dave and Freda Wyatt will be attending another Hog roast there, in aid of funds for the St Mellons show, of which Mr Richards is the president, which is planned for July 16th 2006, a Sunday.

The last hog roast, in the company of Dave and Freda, Jeannette and I had a lovely day, during which Dave and I went for a ramble around the fields and chatted about how the farm had changed over the past 60 years, hopefully I will get to go back to revisit the old place again, in the future, who knows..............

Chapter Eight

Coed-y-Ferm Farm, "Fired", and home again........

At the beginning of my employment with Mr Kelly, at Ty Hir Farm, I had no idea just where the Wyatts had gone to live, but talking to Tony Edwards during his re emergence with Mr Johnny Wintour, back at the farm, I discovered that they had gone to live in the small village of Llangwm, just three miles outside Usk on the road to Chepstow, where they had taken over the tenancy of a small farm, on the Curre Estate, Lady Curre being a noted landowner in that area, who also had a pack of fox-hounds in her name, I believe these animals are noted for their colour and pedigree.

Initially I wrote to the Wyatt family to enquire after their welfare, and in due course I had a nice letter back, inviting me to visit them sometime, and with that I telephoned them and arranged a visit for the following weekend.--- Over the ensuing months I visited them a number of times, and I used to look forward eagerly to my visits to the farm which was called Coed-y-Ferm Farm.

At the auction at Ty Hir, Mr Wyatt had bought the set of disc harrows, but had omitted to take the spare bearings he had purchased during his time as bailiff there, and one evening during my visits, which by now, incidentally had become "long" weekends, these "bearings" had become a topic of conversation, and I said that I would endeavour to bring them with me the next visit, I had not realised just what I was letting myself in for, when I made that promise!!.

I managed to smuggle the said bearings, which were cast-iron and heavy, there were four all-together, and rather awkward, and would just fit into a leather carrier bag, I borrowed from Mam. I put them in this bag and had to walk across four fields from Ty Hir to our home at Nol Bridge Terrace.

On the Saturday morning I caught the Western Welsh bus from Michaelstone into Newport, where I changed buses and caught the Red and White bus to Twynn Square, Usk, changed buses again to go to Llangwm, and got off at the Bridge Inn, and walked the mile or so to the farm, and though we as a family, had made these types of trips many times over the years, what made this one so memorable, was the rattling and clanging which reverberated around the bus, from under my seat as the bus negotiated the numerous corners on our journey, causing the articles to roll out of my bag, a number of times, much to my embarrassment.

I fully understand how the legendary "Harold Steptoe", felt, being the son of a lowly rag and bone man, I felt like him, what with the clanging and rattling going on under my seat !!!

I have already recounted how I eventually went and lived with the Wyatt family, at Coed-y-Ferm, and initially everything was great, but I had forgotten the fact that I have a tendency to become homesick very quickly, and unfortunately this happened after a few weeks or so,

I moved in with the Wyatt's and had my own room, was treated superbly as one of the family, they even supplied my working clothes, and I then started travelling in the other direction at weekends, going home to visit the family, and my friends, but previous to leaving home I had started going to Roath Boxing club, in Cardiff again, I also started to miss my visits to Thomas, the Mill farm, and as these places began to occupy my thoughts, I'm afraid that my work suffered and I became lazy and disinterested, in my job.

During the early weeks at Coed-y-Ferm, the herd which Mr Wyatt had assembled again, was really beginning to prove what a good farmer he really was, he decided to milk the cattle THREE times daily, at 6am 2pm and again at 10 pm –he would start the first milking at 6am, I would join him at 8.30am, we would then do whatever jobs needed doing during the day, milk at 2pm work till teatime, then often Mrs Wyatt and I would go out and do the 10pm Milking, as Mr Wyatt was often asleep, she was loath to wake him, as he was obviously shattered, having been on his feet since before 6am. And this went on for the remainder of my time at the Wyatts.

In one of my initial weekends staying with the family, I used to sleep on a bed settee in the front room and early one morning. I was woken, by someone knocking on my room door, it was Dave Wyatt, asking me would I please give "them a hand", with a heifer cow, which was having difficulty giving birth to its first calf, I immediately got up, and followed him out to the cowshed, where the vet was carrying out a caesarian operation on the animal, as it lay there, ---- I wont go into details, but I will never forget the scene, or the size of the huge cut, that the vet had made in the animals side, to remove the calf, as the mother lay there, happily chewing the cud, as he did so.

After some months I actually began to feel something of a "loner", more so at weekends, because I had no friends in Llangwm, except the Wyatts, and obviously we didn't "want to be in each others pockets" all the time, Dave Wyatt didn't drink, or smoke, and at first I spent a lot of time in pubs in Usk, and on one occasion, I overstayed my time in the pub, and missed my bus back, and decided to walk home, not realising just how far it was, but I eventually began to realise that it was very much further than I had anticipated, --- when I eventually arrived back at the farm, to this day, I don't know what time it was, but I DO remember that it was a freezing cold evening, the wind was blowing a gale, and I had no sooner got into bed, than it was time to get up again.

I really had become something of a "waster", my work began to deteriorate as well, though I was too thoughtless to realise this, then one evening Mr Wyatt said that his sister, a widow, who owned a big farm in Llangattock Lingoed, , on the other side of Abergavenny, wanted a lad to "live in" and work for her, so although I didn't really want to leave the Wyatts, I agreed to go and check out the place I would be going to live at, if I accepted that job, . He took me to the farm called "Old Court", and I met the man who I would be working with, although Mr Wyatts sister, a Mrs Monica Evans, was actually out when we called.

It was a dull, windy and rainy day when we went there, and no doubt this made the place look more gloomy than it really was, I was NOT impressed but promised the Boss an answer after my home visit that weekend, --I knew I wouldn't be going to "Old Court", but in due course I went home, then returned to Coed-y-Ferm, and on the Monday morning I got up and went out to work as per usual, the" Boss" was milking as I walked into the cowshed and said "Good Morning, and thinking I was showing loyalty, I said that I had decided not to accept the new job, --- whereupon Mr Wyatt replied, that I had better find myself another job anyway, -----He didn't want me either!!!

To say I was surprised, would be an understatement, I was absolutely dumbfounded, and for a week or so as it sunk in, I was stunned, and not exactly knowing just what I would do, as I went through the motions of working, ----Mr Wyatt one day, asked me "How much longer it would be before I moved out?.....I consequently packed my bags and moved back to live with Mam and Dad, who had by this time moved to No 17 Hillside Crescent, on the High Cross Estate at Rogerstone.

Some years ago, I was surprised to see an advert in the Press about the forthcoming auction sale at Coed-y-Ferm Farm, the owner, Mr Wyatt was retiring from farming. But thinking about it and realising how farming has changed I realised that even a man like Dave Wyatt deserves a rest, --I have since, on many occasions sat, drank tea, and enjoyed chatting to both Dave and Freda Wyatt, who had a lovely house built in the village of Llangwm, named Pontycaith House, --they are never very far from my thoughts at any time, I value their friendship very much.........

Chapter Nine

Home again, into Industry, and meeting Management.........

I returned home in late 1958 to live with the family, who had by this time, moved to No17 Hillside Crescent on the High Cross Estate, in Rogerstone, and after a week or so of worrying, I obtained work with the other male members of the family, who were already working at Cambrian United Dairies Ltd, at their Marshfield Depot, . Dad, Arthur, David and Noel, were already employed there, and I was put to work with David, and other men, on the "back deck", unloading dirty bottles from delivery lorries, -- the crates containing the bottles were in stacks, and with a truck, we were unloading them, and putting them onto conveyors to go into the plant to be washed and refilled, to emerge from the other side of the building, full of milk to go straight back onto other lorries and delivered to other destinations, Yes I was finding out all about the milk industry, from a completely new perspective.

The work wasn't hard, and by no stretch of the imagination, could it be deemed as mentally challenging either, just rather boring and tedious, but I slowly began to settle into working in a much bigger environment, and having to obey order and formalities, I also had to adhere to the "No Smoking" regulations, which were more difficult to get used to. It did introduce me to industrial life, and also it introduced management to the young Bob Bassett, I settled and after a few months

I was lucky enough to get a job as a "drivers mate", on the Transport Department at the dairies

My new duties, entailed shift work, which was a completely new concept to me, there were only two "mates", myself and another lad, named Jimmy Arundel and we swapped duties on alternate weeks, one week I would be on "Schools" in and around Cardiff, starting at 6am which took about 4 hours, in the afternoon I would then assist another driver on an ordinary bottle delivery load, and the following week, I would be on the "Sterry run", "the school run" would be assisting a driver named, Vince Lewis, and to get to the depot by 6am I would have to make my way to the"Tredegar Arms" pub in Bassaleg, where I would get a lift with two other drivers, John Samuals, and Stan Hicks, who lived in the area and parked the vehicle overnight at the pub car park, but because, I had started drinking and staying out late at nights, I often would often oversleep, and miss my lift, with the result that I became unpopular with management, and received warnings and reprimands about my lack of reliability.

The other driver we would go with regularly, was a certain, Norman Bristow, who sported an Errol Flynn moustache, and ALWAYS appeared immaculately dressed, even though he worked at top speed, he never seemed to get work soiled. He was a big supporter of all German technology, and also married a German girl, and called his house in Greenway Road Rumney, on the outskirts of Cardiff, "Rhineland".!!!

Vince Lewis was a stout little man, who reminded me of a bulldog, but I did enjoy the job although the vehicles in those far off days weren't luxurious like they are today, and I can still visualise the cold wet streets of Cardiff and the steps we had to ascend, to deliver to the various schools of the city, it would be cold and dark at the beginning of the "run", but having completed the deliveries, would come "the reward", when we would go to a small transport café, near to Roath Park, where we would buy a hot mug of tea, and fresh "cheese cobs"---the main feature of this establishment were the large number of caged parrots, which lined the room, these birds would repeat things that customers had said earlier, so that even when only Vince and I were there the place actually sounded busy, with the birds mimicking things they'd heard previously. I doubt this situation would exist today, with rules and health regulations which abound these days

The Drivers Mate's job at the Dairies, had one stipulation, in that, on attaining the full age of 21 years old, I had to take my driving test, conducted by Mr Leonard Webb, the deputy Transport Manager of Cambrian United Dairies, who surprisingly was a fully qualified examiner, failure would mean reverting to the internal staff, and consequently when my turn came to learn to drive, I was allowed to "put my L plates up" under tuition of the drivers I assisted, Class one driving licences allowed a driver to drive articulated vehicles also

Most days Vince Lewis would allow me to put my plates up, and drive the vehicle back to Marshfield along the coast road through St Brides Wenloog all the way back to Marshfield, which was much more demanding than along the main Cardiff/Newport road, because it was only a single lane road, and of course meeting a vehicle entailed one or the other, giving way, or reversing to a passing spot.. After a couple of weeks of instruction my turn to take my test arrived, and it was with some trepidation that I reported to the Transport Office, to face the ordeal. The driving test was not the main problem, Mr Webb was !!, --- he was rather a stern faced individual, who wore horn rimmed glasses, and no-one quite knew how to take him .

On the morning of the Test, surprisingly I was feeling fairly confident, having been out with a number of different drivers, and received lots of encouragement from them all, but when Mr Webb climbed into the vehicle, my nerves failed me, and about two hours later, SO DID HE !!

It was necessary for me to re-take and hopefully, pass my test in a couple of months, and when the fateful day arrived again, I prepared, by popping into the local "Balaclava Inn", for a couple of swift "pints", some cheese and onion sandwiches, hoping that the food would hide the smell of beer, that I had drunk, to sooth my frayed nerves, I climbed into the cab of the vehicle resigned to whatever fate befell me.

We left the Depot with the lorry loaded with a large gantry, and I was surprised when Mr Webb ordered me to drive to Trevethin, a village near Pontypool, which to anyone who knows the area, will agree, that it isn't the easiest place to negotiate due to hills and narrow streets. I can't remember much about the journey, but I was elated when Mr Webb said that although my driving left a lot to be desired, he would pass me!!!--- the next day I became a fully fledged Dairy driver, when I took my first loaded vehicle to Cardiff to do deliveries, in and around the city, --- a day I'll never forget, the cab of the vehicle seemed huge, I had never actually sat for long on my own or driven without the reassuring voice of one of the older and experienced drivers, -- either telling me to slow down, or do this or that, it certainly was a day to remember., ---I could hardly keep the vehicle straight as it roared along the main Cardiff/ Newport road.

During my time at the Dairies, I built myself something of a reputation, which wasn't particularly good, and stemmed from my bouts of excessive drinking, , amongst other things was my habit of getting inebriated at the annual staff dinner and dance, held at the Bindles Ballroom in Barry, South Wales, and on one occasion I lurched, for all the wrong reasons, and fell drunkenly against a lady, who on impact, with a nearby wall, suffered a badly broken arm !!!. She was the wife of a certain Mr Ray Jones, who just happened to be one of my superiors, a Traffic Foreman, -- it seemed that almost every year I would unfortunately be involved in some unsavoury incident, until one year the Transport Manager, summoned me to his office and warned me that he would be supervising that years forth-coming event, and that I had better BEHAVE !, --Mr Wright was a very pleasant man, but wasn't to be crossed, --"NUFF SAID !, I was HAVED, !!!

It was during this period that my drinking career was at its highest, I was a fully fledged member of the firms skittles team, in and around

Cardiff, although I wasn't really interested in the competition, I did enjoy the socialising involved, particularly the beer and the after-match cheese and pickled onions etc. On one occasion, I over did it somewhat, and ended up, late at night, in Cardiff with a couple of the lads, including one Derek Bennett, --- my bus had gone, so Derek, or" Knocker" as he was known, invited me to stay the night at his home.

Derek, actually lived with his widowed mother, in a rented apartment in the Grangetown area of the city, and as we entered the building, he asked me to be as quiet as possible, because their landlady, one of a pair of elderly spinsters, might not be too happy about me staying on the premises, and that they may object, --- dear reader, They most certainly did!!!

That night was unforgettable, in as much as Derek told me to get into bed, and that he would"just pop downstairs" to explain to the landlady that I was his brother, -- everything would be fine, --he said he wouldn't be long!!! I can, dear reader, assure you that, that night was truly remarkable, due to Derek and his mother, arguing with the two landladies, for hours downstairs !!!---over my being there!! I could hear raised voices now and then, -- then a noise on the stairs, a door would slam, --- silence!!, ------ then the voices would start again, ---I had visions of the door bursting open, and one of the old ladies lunging at me with a knife, or something, Thankfully nothing happened, I fell asleep, and left early next day without waiting for breakfast !!!

On another occasion, elder brother Arthur, Derek, and I, decided to go camping in Scotland, a real "spur of the moment decision", Derek had just bought a brand new Austin A35 green van, so we hired a tent from a shop on Cardiff road, Newport, borrowed a primus stove, saucepan, frying pan, blankets and other odds and ends from Mam, -- and off we went, and though I can't remember our route, I know we spent a few nights in Blackpool, Glasgow, Edinburgh and returned home via Coventry, where we watched a game with Newport County, and the lasting image of the Forth Bridge was unforgettable, also Edinburgh was a terrific place with the Castle floodlit as we walked along Princes Street in the early evening.

We went to a variety show at the Princes Theatre in Glasgow, and though the audience were "in stitches" at the antics of the comedian ????--none of us could understand a word of his strong Scottish accent, and it was a really boring evening for us. We had pitched our tent in a field on the outskirts of the city, and proceeded into town, where "everyone will be dressed in kilts, and you will have to order a pint with a whiskey chaser", or so we were told!!!-------when in actual fact, the pubs were closing at 9.30pm and I cant remember seeing anyone in a kilt, and as for the drinking, the miserable looking people and the city of Glasgow certainly never did anything to make or even allow us to enjoy our visit, -- we were glad to leave the place. I did enjoy our camping trip, and as often happens we did have an enjoyable break, though we hadn't planned anything beforehand. Unfortunately on one evening we pitched our tent in a field and went into town, but couldn't find the tent on our return, until we stumbled across it accidentally.--hours later.

I did enjoy my time with Cambrian United Dairies, at Marshfield, where I worked with drivers who included, Vince Lewis, Charlie McClean, Doug Chard, Jack Gamlin, Walter Fudge, Gwyn Barr, Don Forster, Derek Davies, Derek Bennett, Ron Wigmore, and Eddie Myers, (fathers and sons) John Samuals, Johnnie Wall, Harry Renwicks, Alec Underwood, Norman Bristow, George Leonard, Stan Hicks, Harold Phillips, Joe Bracchi, Jimmy Arundel, Bert Hall, Roy(Dropper)Taylor, under the supervision of Traffic Foremen, Reg Ling, Ray Jones and Bill Green, though Stan Hicks was promoted to Foreman at a later date also,

I actually alternated between C.U.D and B.W Rees and Son, who were the main hauliers for the dairies, -- in fact I had three different terms of employment with each company, the main problem with driving for the CUD, was the unsociable hours, such as deliveries of milk late evenings on weekends etc, --- Rees's were, job and finish, collections only, by about midday, but that was seven days a week, and having to get up every morning at 6am, after a heavy night wasn't easy so I did tend to swap jobs if the mood took me, I had also taken to going to Roath Boxing club, and of course the work did interfere with that too. So the reader will maybe understand, why both jobs seemed OK depending on my social requirements at the time.

It is now July 6th 2007, and we now have an old school friend, actually living opposite us in Winchester Close, his name is Ralph Pearce, a year or so older than me, he is married to a young lady who also worked at Cambrian United Dairies at that time, her name was Audrey Pugh, who lived in Coedkernew and with whom we attended Sunday school at the little hall in that village, in those far-off days, she was known as "Little Audrey" when we worked at the Dairies, and Ralph her husband, has been friends with Doug Chard for years, and often visited him in the home where he has been a long time patient over the past years suffering from worsening Dementia.

Graham Rees, of B.W Rees and son Ltd, has had a long battle with cancer, and sadly he passed away on Thursday December 17th 2010

The Bassett Family: Grandfather Albert and Grandmother Emma and their children who lived at Little Farm, West Nash, near Newport Monmouthshire. My father David is seated on floor in front row

My father, David Sidney Bassett aka Bob

My father and mother 'Bob' and Doris Bassett. Taken at a Cambrian United Dairies Staff dance at Bindles Ballroom in Barry, South Wales.

My eldest brother, Arthur and his wife Verlie,
son Julian and daughter Mandy at their home

My older brother David

My elder brother David (wearing white shirt) at work

Photo taken at St Mellons Agricultural Show on Wednesday, 16th March 1950.
Also pictured are my parents, older brother Arthur and younger sister Margarette.
I had just come out of Llandow Hospital and was wearing my new mac.

My younger brother Noel and his wife Christine at Cwrt Bleddyn Hotel 1970

Richard Plaisted, Mam and my younger sister Wendy

Wedding of younger sister Margarette to Alan Benest with daughter Emma, bridesmaid

Younger sister Carol, Mam, younger brother Noel and his wife Christine

Chapter Ten

I could have been a contender, Charlie !!!!

During the early years, organised entertainment was conspicuous by its absence in the Bassett house, this is not a complaint, just a fact, probably because we were after-all, a growing family, the first four children being boys, and we had no problem entertaining ourselves, one of us would have probably heard something in passing, or our enthusiasm being roused by listening to "the big fight" on the wireless. The fact was we were always on tenterhooks wondering if we would have enough"battery" to hear all of the fight, --- before the power faded, and the broadcast likewise, this made the sport seem so unattainable, and was probably the reason why I got hooked on boxing.

The occasion which first imprinted boxing on my life, was in 1946, when our "idol", Bruce Woodcock, the British Heavyweight champion, fought an American named Joe Baksi, and was K.Oed in the fourth round, and sustained a badly broken jaw in the process, it was also at this time that I remember being entered in a fête, being dressed, or rather undressed, as a boxer, standing on a trailer., being pulled by a tractor, through the streets of Usk, in a carnival., I say our idol, because in those early days, eldest brother Arthur, was more "au fait" with the personalities of sport, and don't forget, that unlike me he was at the time a budding teenager, and a high school pupil to boot!!

From then on, boxing always interested me, but I usually followed Arthur who was the authority on sport in our house, David was only interested in football, but I can vividly recall Arthur and I having some tremendous "world title fights", --- wearing socks on our hands, for gloves, ----Arthur would "do" a running commentary, while he proceeded to "outpoint me" !!----I don't ever recall" winning ", but Arthur would make me "sound" good, in his commentary, and winning didn't seem to matter anyway.

We followed our idols from a distance in those early days, we didn't see many newspapers, in fact hardly any, except when we lived at Llancayo, when we would wait for ages in Usk town for the Football Argus to arrive, after we had earlier watched Usk Town play on their home ground "The Island", situated alongside the River Usk in the town, -- though why we waited for the paper seems a bit silly, as it obviously would be quite a while before it was ready, but we did enjoy the fish and chips with vinegar, while we waited outside the "The Bazaar", as the paper shop was called in those days.

Any big sporting occasion was usually shown during the following week on the Newsreel in local cinemas, and on rare occasions we managed to go to the "pictures", though we did have a smaller version of the cinema at "The Red Shed", a corrugated building, situated on the roadside in close proximity to the Usk R.F.C sports field, and I can vaguely recall seeing highlights of Freddie Mills fighting Gus Lesnevitch, an American World Light-heavyweight Champion, unfortunately we had to sit in the cheap seats, which resulted in our view being distorted, and made it difficult to enjoy the spectacle, because everything seemed to be on a steep slope, as we gazed up at the huge screen about eight feet up and away from us,

I eventually got involved in amateur boxing when I was about fourteen and had discovered that there was a boxing club in the Roath area of Cardiff, the gym was in a lock up premises in Nora Street off Broadway, in the city and with my meagre pocket money, earned on the bakers van, and the paper round, I managed to visit the club occasionally and got a tremendous "kick" when I realised some of the people I was mingling with, --- I WAS actually in the same room as Trevor Snell, the Welsh amateur Heavyweight Champion, and Gordon Blakey, the Featherweight Champion, and they actually spoke to ME!!

I used to travel by bus from Castleton, to the "Royal Oak Hotel", on the city outskirts, and walk along Broadway to the club, unfortunately my visits were not often and my kit was, shorts and "daps", until the day arrived when I had saved enough to buy proper ring boots, and the other kit I needed, ie, gum shield and bandages etc.

I actually had five bouts spread over about eighteen months, winning four, although they were only with lads who were mostly members of the several clubs, in and around Cardiff, namely Victoria Park and St Clares boxing clubs, and took place in either our club, or at the other two, usually put on to raise funds for new equipment, and I actually found out about, and visited the professional gymnasium, called"England's Gym ", situated in Customs House Street, near to Cardiff General station, which was run by the legendary Mr Benny Jacobs, where I met my idol, Joe Erskine, who was later to become the British and Empire Heavyweight champion, and where I later got to spar with many of the lesser known professionals, sometimes at the Roath club, and later at England's gym.

It was during one of my frequent visits to England's gym, that I met a young Nigerian, named Hogan Bassey, who was frequenting the gym to "work out", until he moved away to the midlands, and later signed with the man who eventually guided him to become the World Featherwight champion, Mr George Biddles, and it was at this time in 1957 that he came back to visit and thank the people, who had made him so welcome, when he was new into this country, he gave us signed photographs, and I still have mine!!!.

In 1958 I then had the opportunity to go to live and work for Mr Wyatt, at Llangwm, near Usk, and my interest was diverted away from the sport for some time, I should perhaps point out that it was difficult to get involved with amateur boxing, because as far as I knew there didn't seem to be a lot of information, or publicity about it in those days, and it was pretty discouraging, and easy to get disillusioned with the lack of response to ones efforts, which seemed apparent.

When I went to work at the Dairies, or rather some weeks before, I had revisited Roath Boxing club, and had become friendly with the trainer, a man named Billy Manning, a dour greying, ginger haired man, who asked me where I had been hiding since I last visited the club, some seven months earlier, I explained my movements and reasons for not having been to the club, and mentioned my disappointment at my apparent failure to create interest, by my efforts, during the rounds of sparring I had been doing earlier, and he replied, that he HAD "noticed me", but that his way of working was to keep a watching brief, that when I had satisfied his standards, he would do all he could to see that I got regular contests, when I was ready, his reply DID encourage me somewhat!!

In the late 50's I and a number of mates from Rogerstone were on a coach trip to Weston super Mare, and during a meal at a seaside restaurant, I learned that the said establishment was owned by one of British boxing's greatest legends, the former World Flyweight champion, Jimmy Wilde, a legend in his own lifetime, who weighed barely eight stone, but who often fought men two and sometimes three stone heavier than himself, and who had gone unbeaten for over 120 contests!! I had a long conversation with the little man, but some days later I was shocked to read that he had been mugged and beaten up by three drunks, and hospitalised in a serious condition, Sadly he never recovered and died shortly afterwards, I have spoken to one of his relatives who lives in Newport in 1998 following a story I read in the South Wales Argus.

It was purely by coincidence that I got back into boxing, I had been out drinking and playing skittles for the Dairies team, in and around Cardiff, and as usual I was making my way back to the General Station, to get my bus home, slightly the worse for drink, and in company with my mate Jimmy Arundel, we decided to buy a paper from the news-stall which was situated in the passageway under Astey's Restaurant, and the proprietor heard Jimmy using bad language, and asked him to stop, whereon we had a bit of a confrontation with the man, who claimed that he actually controlled all the professional boxers in the Principality............I thought, I don't think so!!! and I asked him who he was?, ...it transpired that his name was Mr Billy Davies, the secretary of the Welsh Boxing Board of Control whereupon, I immediately challenged him to prove it by assisting me to "get into" the professional game. He proved his credentials by arranging for me to participate in a number of "trial bouts" a week or so later at the England's gymnasium owned by Benny Jacobs, who was at that time second only to Jack Solomons, as the top manager in British professional boxing, the gym was at the time situated above the fruit warehouses, in Customs House Street, a stones throw from the general station.

It was with some trepidation that I arrived at England's Gym on the arranged day, and even more nervous when I climbed the stairs leading to the gym, and entered the large room, and recognised the number of well-known fighters "working out", and sparring in the large ring, I recognised Joe Erskine, the British Heavyweight champion, Phil Edwards, who had two tremendous bouts with Terry Downes, the World Middleweight champion, and numerous other well known professionals, all hard at work at various exercises around the room, I was greeted by Billy Davies, who I had met some weeks earlier who introduced me to the small bespectacled Benny Jacobs, and the reason for my being there, was explained by Mr Davies.

Ernie Hurford, a bald elderly man, who was the head trainer, (Archie Rule was Joe Erskine's own trainer) looked after the gym and gave the orders, told me to get changed, and "gloved up", which I did somewhat nervously, I then had the "dubious pleasure, of boxing three, three minute rounds with a well muscled middleweight named Eddie Bee, who had the comical habit of pulling his gum shield back into his mouth, by hooking his tongue under it, ---I didn't have time to be concerned, at the end of the third round, I had a new opponent, a small featherweight named David(Darkie) Hughes, who sometime later fought for the British title, held by Dave Charnley, and if that wasn't sufficient, at the end of the sixth round I was given a thorough going over for three more rounds, by a welterweight named Teddy Best, a man who after a long career as a professional, himself, was later to become even more well known as the manager of Steve Robinson, who won the World championship too. I think I made quite a good impression with the watching professionals, because I got a good round of applause at the end, I later signed what was, in those days, known as a Boxer/Manager Agreement, with Mr Jacobs, who told me to get fit, "and we'll see what we can arrange"

I'm afraid that this is where I let myself down, by not"knuckling down" to hard work, to get fit and learn, as advised, and though I did enjoy a number of memorable occasions, still as an amateur, over the ensuing years, and though I now look back with regrets, and I DO believe that, had I shown the dedication required, I could have done very well.......buts that's life !!!

In 1958 at the age of twenty, I was training at England's gym, where I became quite friendly with amongst others, Joe Erskine, who was at that time the British and Empire Heavyweight champion, who, although I was only an amateur, allowed me to borrow his gloves and equipment, because I always had a problem finding gloves big enough to get my hands into. Whenever I went to the gym, I always got a special "buzz" walking up the long dark stairway which led from the street level, up two floors, to the half glass door of the gym, because of the rhythmic noises emanating from within, ---the sound of the corner ties of the ropes, rattling against the corner posts, skipping ropes slapping on the floor surface, and leather against leather of the heavy punch-bag, intermingled with "snorts" of exertion of big fellows sparring-----shouts of "last ten!!" and then the clang of the bell to signal the end of a "round"---------everything in a boxing gym is done in three minute rounds timing. Its an atmosphere I cant explain, but I loved it, and even now as I type, I can still "hear" it, but then I've always said that"I'm boxing mad!!"

In late 1958 Joe Erskine, who was making a return to the ring after a disastrous one round K.O defeat to a giant Cuban named Nino Valdez, was training to defend his titles against Brian London, had moved his training down the road to the Roath Boxing Club gym, and a number of us had volunteered to assist Archie Rule and Benny Jacobs with some of the menial work, like tidying up after work outs etc and it was whilst helping here, as often as we could in the evenings, I only managed once or twice a fortnight, due to work rota, only managing it when I was on the early morning school run, But I was lucky enough to be there when Tommy Farr, who actually fought Joe Louis, in America in 1937, called in to interview Joe, and to "cover" Joe's training for "The News of the World" newspapers.

I was also fortunate enough to have the opportunity to "spar" with a young Nigerian boxer named Hogan Bassey, who was newly arrived in this country, but who was considered very talented and actually went on to win the World Featherweight Title under the guidance of George Biddles a top midland manager, Hogan later sent a number of signed photographs to the gym as a thank you to the people who had made him so welcome I still have my copy.

On a trip to Wembley to see the World Speedway Championships, with my mate Frank Young we made a short detour, and found Henry Cooper's large greengrocery shop near the stadium, Henry was actually serving customers, and I was thrilled to say "Hello", even though my idol Joe Erskine was later "robbed" of his title by the referee Eugene Henderson, in the fight with Henry Cooper., --- the decision was so bad Henderson never refereed another contest.

In 1960, I joined the 1st The Queen's Dragoon Guards, for a period of nine years, which may appear to be a large step to take, but the fact was it was a choice of either six or nine years, so I reasoned that if I could do six years, I would or should be well used to service life, and three more would be OK, and as things turned out I enjoyed the life for a while, but with my home sickness history I had my doubts, so deciding it would be better to be safe than sorry, I resigned while it was still possible to get my release on payment of £20 pounds within four months, one day longer and the price rocketed, elder brother David sent me the necessary cash, and I think I still owe him for it.

While I was in uniform, I entered and won the regimental championship of the Royal Armoured Corps, whilst stationed at Barnard Castle, in County Durham, during which I had three hard contests to reach the final, in which I was due to meet the reigning champion, a Corporal Billy Turner, at a large tournament a week later----he had a tremendous reputation, and I was encouraged to "do your best, but don't take a hammering"!!!, -- if I needed an incentive, that was it!, I was determined that no one was going to "hammer" me, and after four rounds of blood and thunder action, I received the unanimous decision of the judges, and Turner, who had rather a prominent nose, received the attention of the doctor, because of the damage I had done to him.

During the following weeks, I received very much improved treatment from my superiors, and a number of promises of "stripes", and "cushy jobs", if I transferred to one of several other regiments to box, -- but I stuck to my plans and came home.

Some months later, I was visiting a fairground at Shaftsbury Park in Newport, with my mates and, for "a laugh", I decided to "have a go" in a boxing booth, where I won five pounds for lasting three rounds with a rather paunchy old "boxer", I hadn't realised it, but I was reported to the Welsh ABA, and received a five year ban, for accepting money, while still officially only an amateur, I appealed and was reinstated after ten months, because in those days it was a "hanging offence" even to speak to a professional, let alone accept money, other than travel expenses, if you were very lucky.!!

In 1961, I had been training at Joe Carr's gym in Commercial Road, in Newport, and Mr Carr suggested that it would be a good idea to try for a W.A.B.A championship, prior to turning professional, to give myself some bargaining power, so it was decided that I would enter the championships at middleweight as an unattached competitor, and I continued to train at the gym and sparring with one of Mr Carr's, sponsored immigrants, a coloured lad named Kennarth Sengal, who spoke very little English, but who insisted that his name, was as spelt above, and definitely not shortened.

Joe Carr was well known for sponsoring foreign boxers into Britain and eventually obtaining professional licences for them, but on this occasion, we had been boxing only a matter of minutes, when I caught Kennarth with a glancing blow, but split his cheek rather badly, the remainder of the afternoon was spent in "Casualty" at the "Gwent", getting stitches in his injury.

I entered the Welsh Senior Championships which were held at the Drill Hall, Dumfries Place in Cardiff, in March 1961, as a middleweight, which in those days was 11 stone 11 pounds, though I don't know what that equates to in today's weights of kilograms and the like, and when I arrived at the venue, I was to put it mildly, rather nervous, I walked in through the blue double doors and was surprised to find myself in a large spacious building, with two immaculate rings, side by side, with about ten feet of space between them, tiers of seating filled the hall with a row of tables along one side of each ring to accommodate the time keeper and judges, I wondered how on earth the fighters would distinguish the start and finish of the rounds being so close together, -- I would have the opportunity to find out soon enough!!!

I tried to appear casual and look as if I "belonged" there, but really I had no idea what the procedure was, all I knew was that I had a card in my pocket, which had arrived in the mail days ago, which informed me that I had to report at 11am to officials of the W.A.B.A, to undergo a medical examination, and to weigh. After a short while, I began to relax and take stock of my surroundings, I noticed in one corner of the hall what looked like a lot of activity, so I walked across and found that there was a large notice board, with a time-table of the tournament's events, and to one side, I saw a notice above the door which said, "Boxers/Trainers", with that I walked through and found myself in what was obviously the communal dressing room.

I found a vacant area and sat down on the bench which ran the length of the room, another one was also on the other side of the room, and they were rapidly filling up as people entered loaded with kit bags etc. It was approaching 10.45am, and my card had stated 11am, so I decided to get changed into my kit, I could see a couple of scales, and queues were forming to see the two men armed with stethoscopes, who were obviously the doctors.

I was feeling a bit "lost", as I knew that I needed a "second" to work in my corner, in any contests that I would be participating in, and as yet, I hadn't spotted anyone that I knew, who I could call upon. The room was, by now, getting really crowded, as boxers from all areas of the Principality were in the process of preparation for participating in a what was a very busy programme of bouts from "flyweight", right up to a number of "hefty" looking heavyweights,

I was beginning to panic a bit, when I noticed on the far side of the room, the familiar face of Bill Manning, From the Roath Boxing club, and I made a beeline to him, and said "Hello", and he looked surprised to see me, and even more so, when I told him that I was boxing that day, because, it is usual for the club trainer to put people forward for championships, but he did agree to assist me, if he wasn't involved in other contests, and he also assured me that he would make sure I had someone in my corner, come what may, ---which was very reassuring!!!.

I waited in line, to see the doctors, there were a large number of boxers, many of them had been through this routine at other big tournaments, whereas at the small shows I had been on previously, there were usually only about twenty or thirty lads, and a few trainers, nothing like this lot!!---when I got to the scales, I stepped on, the official in charge, asked me my name, and weight, and looking down at the scales, seemed a bit surprised, and suggested that I "go down" a weight to Light Middleweight, because I was actually below 11stone 2pounds, the limit for that weight, I replied "Thanks but I'll stay as I am at middleweight", with that I stepped off the scales, and stood as the doctor examined my chest, and poked a light in my ear-hole, signed my medical card, and said "Next", --- I was ready!!!

I went back to my spot in the dressing room and sat for about three quarters of an hour, I could tell by the noise outside, in the hall that the bouts had started, then I enquired and was told that the "Lists" were up on the board, in the outer room, so I joined the crowd of boxers and trainers gathered around the notice board, and scanned the list of names, until I spotted R Bassett(Unattached) v S Price, Cwmmer Afon B.C . Ring No1. 13.45, I then knew that I had just over half an hour to wait. Trying to appear, nonchalant, I decided to try to find out who "S Price" was, and asking around I discovered that he was rather a tall youthful lad, with a schoolboy parting in his hair, and my confidence rocketed, and I began to have visions of at least one good victory, there were only eleven boxers in the middleweight division, so my chances seemed quite promising.

Over the ensuing minutes, I experienced a number of different emotions as the atmosphere and tension grew, --the door would open and fighters and trainers would enter, either the worse for wear, and raging over "that bastard ref'", or beaming after a good win, then someone yelled, "Bassett, Price, Come on !!"---I stood up and looked across at Bill Manning, who picked up his canvas bag and motioned me to follow him.

Feeling slightly apprehensive I followed my friend, who had been through this procedure many times over the years, as we walked down the side of the hall to steps of the left hand ring many thoughts were flashing through my mind, --- watch I don't miss a step on the climb up to the ring, it would be just like me to trip!!!...........Bill climbed the steps and I followed, --- the ring seemed quite large, and there seemed a good crowd in the hall, though it was early in the tournament, there followed a haze of action I just cant really remember, apart from the fact that, the bell signalled the start of the contest, and my education began, !! S Price, the youngish looking schoolboy was in fact, Stuart Price, a superb experienced "southpaw" boxer, who landed many punches during the three rounds, I just couldn't get past his right glove, or out of the way of it----for that matter !--------Price, was the Welsh answer to Scotland's Dick McTaggart, a supreme craftsman, and though I did give him a good contest, I lost by a unanimous decision of the judges

I had been well beaten, but I wasn't down hearted, because I knew I had been in with a top-class fighter, I showered and dressed, but due to the punches I had taken during the bout, which at the time, I had been too busy to really notice, my nose was slightly the worse for wear, and just wouldn't stop bleeding, I said my good byes, and thanked Mr Manning, and said I would see him at the Roath club, ---- left to go home. I caught the bus, and found a seat and sat down, during my journey home, my time was spent answering people who were enquiring, "What on earth has happened to you, my love?----Have you been mugged?"----I bet Henry Cooper never got asked questions like that!!!

In the ensuing years I boxed in another three Welsh Championships, and actually had three contests with the then Welsh Amateur Heavyweight Champion.-- one Maldwyn Isaacs, a member of the "Semtex Boxing club", in Brynmawr, the first was at the Underwood Social club, Llanmartin, which was a bit like a World title fight atmosphere, in that people were so eager to see the bout that they were actually standing on tables, because the village had never seen any live boxing, never mind a Welsh Champion in their midst before!!.........Maldwyn turned professional shortly after our third contest and went on to have quite a successful professional career.

I then fought him for the second time at Pontnewynydd working-men's club, and the third time was at Pontypridd Town Hall, we had three terrific scraps, but I never managed to beat him, although I always conceded over a stone in weight, he never put me on the floor once, --in fact, only one man did, his name was Jimmy Verstappen, a Dutchman, though I did take a standing count of "eight", in a contest at the Marina club, on Penarth pier, on Monday May 23rd 1966, when I was boxing in an Empire Games, selection tournament, and lost, when the referee stopped the contest half way through the second round, on that occasion I "know" I would have beaten my opponent, but typical of poor standard refereeing by an official who had never laced a glove on, he jumped in and stopped the contest, even though I hadn't taken a decent punch, my opponent was rushing in with arms flailing, the so called official was so impressed and stopped the fight, worse still he robbed me of a place in the Welsh team, for the forth coming Empire Games, which if my memory serves me correct, were due to take place in Edinburgh later that same year.

It was also in 1970 that I fought the lad who was at heavyweight for Wales, v's Holland, we met at the Tonyrefail Labour club, and I got a points decision, In October of that same year I boxed on a show at the Aneurin Labour club, in Trethomas, which if my memory serves me correctly, was otherwise known as the "Green Fly", don't ask me why, -- I fought a man named Alex Manley, a member of Newport Sporting club, and I literally won every round, but to my disgust, and that of the crowd, they awarded the decision to Manley, although I continued in the sport for some years, as a judge/referee and timekeeper, I think that was my last contest, --what hurt most wasn't the loss, but the report in the South Wales Argus, that stressed the fact that Manley had come back from a four year retirement to beat"Welsh International Bob Bassett"-- -------Newport Sporting club always received good "write ups" because their trainers Colin and Glyn Waters actually worked for the paper, in those days, and their father was founder/coach of the Newport Sporting club too.

In 1966 and 1967, whilst training and boxing under the guidance of Noel Trigg, later to become a councillor and Mayor of Newport, who had opened a new gym at Caerwent, near Chepstow, I fought the son of a well respected Newportonian, named Jim Blackborrow, his name was Johnny, he beat me twice on points, the first time in the Welsh A.B.A middleweight championship, in Cardiff on February 19th 1966. Over the ensuing years, my exploits in boxing ranged from quite good to terrible, as I moved from club to club to attempt to make progress and make my mark, in the sport.

One incident summed up the situation, inasmuch, that it's not just a case of being good enough, its often rather a matter of who you know, that counts, let me explain, I was working as a driver in 1960, for a company in Newport, Short Haulage, operating out of their Dock street depot, and at that time, training at Belle Vue boxing club, at the Pill Labour Hall, Newport under the guidance of a man named Charlie Saunders. One evening I arrived home at Hillside Crescent, Rogerstone, and Mam said"Robert, the man from the boxing has been here, they want you to go to France !!" I immediately got back into my vehicle and drove to Baldwin street, Newport, to see Mr Saunders, who confirmed that I had indeed been selected to represent Wales versus France, in Paris in just under three weeks time.

I was feeling absolutely "chuffed", but I was in for a nasty surprise, a the days passed I was training hard and sparred many rounds with a professional middleweight, named Jimmy "Cyclone" Slattery, and I obviously thought that I was getting ready for the "trip", under the watchful eye of Charlie Saunders, we were knocking "six-bells" out of each other. About a week before the "date", Saunders informed me that he was withdrawing me, because he "didn't think I was ready".

I was devastated, and went home.------Two Newport Sporting club, brothers Colin and Glyn Waters, who's father, Walt was the Welsh coach, were at loggerheads with the Welsh A.B.A, for a long time, on the grounds that he considered that BOTH of his sons should be in the Welsh team, they were very good boxers, of that there was no doubt, but that didn't give them a divine right to international honours. I later found out that Charlie Saunders was their relative.

After I got married in 1963, we went to live, first in Caldicot, and then to Underwood Estate, Llanmartin, and it was during our domicile here, that I met the man who was to become a good friend, and to share many pleasant boxing occasions with me over the ensuing years, his name was Charlie Booth, a likeable Cockney, who was actually the manager of a department, in the giant Spencer Steel works at Llanwern, near Newport.. Charlie lived a few streets away from me, and hearing that I was involved in boxing, asked me would I be interested in forming a boxing club on our estate at Llanmartin, I said yes, and in due course the Spencer Works Boxing club was formed and "installed" at the Community Centre, which was actually an old prefab building at Underwood Estate.

Over the ensuing months Charlie used his influence and obtained funding from his employers for equipment, a ring, punch balls, gloves, etc, and also persuaded the council to allow us to use the main hall of the Centre as a gymnasium on certain evenings, free of charge. I was by now working for F Bowles and Sons Ltd as a ready mix lorry driver, and had developed a healthy suntan, with my hair cut, in a very short crew cut, and the ladies, who used to run the lending library, in the adjoining room at the Centre, christened me.----- "Charlie's Golden Boy", and I often had a number of them as onlookers, as I did my "workouts", in the evening-------No.!! there wasn't much entertainment at Underwood Estate, in those days.!!!

Over the past years I had moved to and from a number of different boxing clubs and had achieved varying success, Newport Sporting club, Maindee Boxing club, Belle Vue B.C and of course originally with Roath Youth A.B.C in Cardiff, I also had a period with Noel Trigg at the new gym he had opened at the Coach and Horses Inn at Caerwnt, the home of Caerwent A.B.C, at the same time with my friend Charlie Booth at Spencer Works B.C, where we enjoyed our "15 minutes of Fame" when we represented Wales v Holland, on the nationally televised show, in 1970, in fact it was during my association with Charlie, and Noel Trigg, that I had some marvellous, if slightly daft moments.

Noel Trigg had a very poor memory, and on one occasion we travelled all the way to Wolverhampton, for a show, only to find that it had been cancelled days earlier, on checking his diary, Noel found that he had indeed been notified of this fact, but it had slipped his memory, Charlie Booth was a little Cockney, who had worked his way up to the position of Chairman of the Welsh A.B.A Eastern Division, as well as being a referee and judge. This fact often used to work against me, for example when I was boxing Charlie would sometimes be called upon to officiate, either as a judge or referee, and would ALWAYS vote for the other man---JUST TO PROVE HOW UNBIASED HE REALLY WAS !!!!

Charlie was a lovely man, but he would often book me for contests, and when I enquired who I was due to fight, his reply would be, "Oh, he's only a novice", or "You'll hammer him, Bob !", after the bout, I would often find, by examining my opponent's records, would reveal a completely different story, --Yes everyone liked Old Charlie, but he was so naive!! .

Charlie and I travelled to Barry for a big "Dinner Show" at the Memorial Hall, on Wednesday, January 28th 1970, to discover that the show was not until the next day, the 29th, and when we returned to the venue the following day, I found that I was fighting a lad from the Battersea B.C, who's name was Bob Barrett, he was a coloured boy, and consequently we had a terrific scrap, which I won on points, but the thing I recall about this occasion was that I at the time was sporting long sideburns, and betting on the contests was being allowed, in aid of charity, and during the bout I heard many shouts of "Come on Whiskers", meaning me!!

One of my main problems was lack of actual training partners of my own weight, Charlie and I used to travel to Newbridge B.C and a number of times to Cwmmer Afon B.C, near Bridgend, just to spar with heavyweights, Eddie Roberts the senior Welsh coach, had a son Tony, who fought at heavyweight, on TV the same night as I fought Jimmy Vestappen, the Dutch champion, I fought and got a decision against Tony, on a show at Tonyrefail, about two months later.

I boxed at social clubs all over South and West Wales, Bristol, Totnes and Wolverhampton, twice at the Ebbw Bridge club in Newport, which was at the time about the most popular club of its kind in the Principality, but as I have stated earlier, the biggest night of my career was on Thursday February 12th 1970. I had arrived at the gym in Llanmartin on the Sunday February 8th, for our usual club night, to be met by an excited Charlie, with the news that I had been selected to box for Wales against Holland for "The Joe Carr Cup", at Merthyr on the following Thursday February 12th 1970.

After a succession of spontaneous, gleeful yells and cheers, from both myself and the members of the Spencer Works boxing club, I casually asked Charlie to confirm that it was at heavyweight, , as I was weighing about13 stone 6pounds, comfortably, ---he replied No, its at light heavy, now to the uninformed this would not be a problem, but the fact was that in order to box at light-heavyweight, I would need to shed at least eight pounds in order to scale 12 stone 12 pounds or under, and I had a maximum of FOUR days to achieve this goal!!!

Over the ensuing 3 to 4 days, I starved myself, drank gallons of unsweetened black coffee, which is a recommended method of weight reduction, but when I stepped on the scales in Merthyr at 4pm on the day of the show, I weighed a fraction under 13 stone, and the Dutch officials agreed to allow me an extra two hours to lose the offending poundage, so with that Charlie and I retired to the boiler house at the Hoover works where I put on extra clothing and skipped in close proximity to a large coal fired boiler, and I did manage to sweat it off, with minutes to spare, but I was completely shattered, but resolved to do my best anyway!!

The bout was one of four contests that were being televised by BBC

"Sportsnight with Coleman" and after a face to face interview with the legendary Harry Carpenter, I returned to the dressing room and prepared for what was my big night. Of the fight itself, I can remember little apart from the fact that halfway through round one, I found myself on the canvas, I could see the red light on top of a large TV camera, which was aimed in my direction, and I knew that I had to get up, ----
---and I did. I regained my composure and completed the duration of the bout, but not surprisingly I lost on points, I did represent Wales on several other occasions, but THAT was the big one!!.

At work the next day, whilst driving my ready mix concrete lorry, delivering to a site in Caerphilly, I was approached by a number of workmen, who asked me had I been on TV the previous evening? Doing my best to portray a modest sporting personality, I answered, "Yes, I was", half expecting a request for an autograph or some such request, whereupon the one chap proceeded to tell me that I was "flaming useless" and even went on to describe just how I should have gone about winning the fight, ---- a typical "Armchair Champion"

No, I don't miss being in the spotlight at all, but that's another story.

In 2007, while involved in a project with BBC Wales, I met a young lady named MelanieLindsell who lives in Tintern, and in conversation with her mentioned the TV broadcast, and lo and behold she searched the archives at the BBC and actually unearthed the actual film of the contest and it is now my most treasured possession, to see the bout for the first time some 37 years after the event was a very emotional experience, but I am pleased to say that though I didn't win, I dont think I disgraced myself in any way.

The author after representing Wales v Holland 12th February, 1970

J. VERSTAPPEN
NED. KAMPIOEN 1969 — HALFZWAAR

My opponent, Dutch Light-Heavyweight Champion Jimmy Verstappen

ANNUAL AWARDS

BOB BASSETT

.INTERNATIONAL REPRESENTATIVE

SPECIAL AWARD

CHAIRMAN   R.J.CHAMBERS   8 th SEPTEMBER 2007

SECRETARY   KEN GRAY   8 th SEPTEMBER 2007

A QUITTER NEVER WINS
A WINNER NEVER QUITS

Presented by:- GARY LOCKET (World Professional Middleweight Champion)
on September 8ᵗʰ 2007,------" For Services to Welsh Amateur Boxing".

Award from the Welsh Amateur Boxing Association in 2007 for services to Welsh Amateur Boxing. This was presented to my by Garry Lockett, the W.B.V. World Middleweight Champion at an Eastern Division Awards night in Newport, 8th September, 2007

That Was a Surprise!!.

At the time that I was a member of the Spencer Works Boxing club, or maybe I should say, when I WAS the Spencer Works boxing club, after all, I was the only active member of the club over the age of about twelve or thirteen, all the other members were newly enrolled into what was a new venture on the estate, -----I was selected to represent the the Welsh A.B.A Eastern Division, against the Western Counties A.B.A on a big Dinner Show, being held at the Totnes Town Hall, down in Devon, and I was booked to fight a man called Arthur Tyrell, who was at the time, going great guns, and I knew that I would have to pull out all the stops, to have any chance, Charlie Booth my trainer, wouldn't be in my corner this time, instead I would have the support of the head coach of the Welsh A.B.A, named Eddie Roberts, who was the father of Tony, the heavyweight of that name, this pleased me a lot, because Eddie was a vastly experienced man, who would be a big reassuring help in my corner, and I was looking forward to having him with me, very much.

The show was on the Saturday evening, and the team travelled down on the Friday, by coach, and we would be staying till the Sunday morning, we were installed into our hotel, which was situated at the bottom of a steep hill about half a mile away from the venue.

On the Saturday evening everything was going well and we were ahead by four bouts to two, when my turn came to get into the ring to show them what I could do, and knowing that I had Eddie Roberts to advise me made me feel quite good, I had received a complete set of Welsh kit, Dressing gown Vest, the lot, which made me feel a bit special too, ----------In the first round neither of us did much, apart from throwing and missing with many of our punches, as we tried to get "warmed up" and find our range, and when the bell went I returned to my corner.

I sat down, and Eddie went through the usual routine, half drowning me with cold water from a sponge, ---Charlie was his equal in that department!!. but then he told me that when the bell goes for the second round, to get straight across the ring and to hit him as hard as I could, —to show him I was the BOSS!.

The bell rang!!! and as per my instructions, I charged across, --- fearlessly!!---after all Eddie knew ALL about tactics, and I had every confidence in him!!, I got within hitting distance, and threw my best punch, —unfortunately, I wasn't quite fast enough because I felt a terrific thud, as he hit me, in the middle of my chest, which made me wonder, what the hell I was doing hanging around long enough to let him hit me like that!!

After what seemed like an eternity, I regained my composure, I hadn't "gone down", but though Mr Tyrell hadn't realised it, he had missed a golden opportunity to make his punch "count"---I got to work and at the end of the second round I went back to Eddie, who repeated the procedure with the sponge, and a lot of words and gestures which I didn't feel too inclined to listen to, —my faith in the man was severely "dented"!!!

After an uneventful third round, we waited in the centre of the ring for the decision, which I thought I might have just "shaded" ------the judges thought otherwise, and gave it to my opponent, I guess they were as impressed as I was with the "punch", --it did bloody hurt, at the time.!!

On bigger shows, and when you have been specifically asked to box, it is usual to receive full expenses as well as a "prize" or trophy, but in the early days of ones career, it is just a case of attending shows and trying to get "matched" there and then, but named fighters always get good expenses, and I had been around long enough to be in the known category, and on this occasion I was told to select a prize from the table in the foyer, Jeannette and I were just about"making ends meet", --- and after careful perusal of the aforementioned table, I spotted a beautiful rose patterned bone china dinner service, which I selected as my reward.

We then showered and dressed to meet up in the Dining room, to have what was, a very good meal, which we all enjoyed, followed by the usual speeches by W.A.B.A officials.

After the evening had closed, we checked all our belongings onto the coach and retired to our Hotel rooms to go to bed. we were told to be ready to leave straight after breakfast on the Sunday morning. We duly boarded the coach the following day and on the trip home many of the group were playing cards, but one by one we were called to the front of the coach and given our expenses, though due to it being a weekend we could not claim loss of earnings, so expenses were low, but I comforted myself in the knowledge, that Jeannette would be pleased with my wonderful prize, Hell!!, we'd be practically "posh" with a new china dinner service!!!

We arrived in Newport, and I caught a taxi from the bus station, being careful to collect all my belongings from the coach, and in due course I arrived home, and being eager to show Jeannette our new acquisition, tore open the large brown cardboard box in which it was packed.........I found my prized completely smashed into small pieces, Disappointment was an understatement!!!!!!----I immediately phoned Colin Waters, of the Welsh A.B.A who as mentioned earlier, was also a leading light in the Newport Sporting club, who on hearing my story, assured me that I would in due course receive a complete replacement for the shattered dinner service.

All this took place on March 28th 1970, on a Totnes Rotary Club Dinner show, and I'm still waiting for a replacement Dinner Service –I gather from public opinion that this is one of the more reputable societies, they certainly haven't proved their credentials this time, and I'm beginning to think that if and when I get my replacement dinner service----

   ---THAT WILL BE A SURPRISE !!!

Chapter Eleven

We were in a fine State

You may recall in earlier chapters I mentioned the trip of a lifetime, Jeannette and I made, in 1985, when we visited America, on a country music package tour of the Southern states, culminating in a visit to the White House, in Washington D.C I had become a country music fan as a child listening to a radio show, called "The Big Bill Campbell and his Rocky Mountain Rhythm Band Show," and over the years my musical tastes have ranged from Country music, through the Rock and Roll era, when I ran a fan club in partnership with a lad named Mike Evans from Cardiff, for what was the first big name band to tour Britain in 1954, namely Bill Haley and his Comets.

Since I became interested in computers and the web, I have realised that this media provides me with the perfect means of research into a wide range of topics, and it has given the chance to search for the discography of the aforementioned artistes, and I have now obtained cd's of Big Bill Campbell and his band, which I enjoy as I listen to D.I.Y compilation music tapes in my car. The aforementioned Mike Evans and I met at the Gaumont Theatre Cardiff, at what was the only Welsh "gig" on Bill Haley's first ever tour of Britain.

Bill Haley was, a country singer with his band at that time, "The Saddlemen", his speciality being "yodelling", prior to his forming a new band, "The Comets", and releasing a ground-breaking new sound, —Rock and Roll, with the release of "Rock the Joint", some years later

I joined !The British Country-music Association" which I was able to do, after having two songs arranged and put on tape, by a professional singer from the West Country named "Rambling" Mal Daron, and it was through the BCMA's offer to members, of a twenty two days holiday tour of principal country music sites in the USA, at the "snip" of a cost of £650.00 per person.

Having never travelled abroad before, or since for that matter, the furthest I had been was to Scotland on a camping trip with Arthur and Derek "Knocker" Bennett, mentioned in an earlier chapter, I was a bit apprehensive, to say the least, a fear of heights didn't help, and my imagination was in "overdrive, conjuring up visions too frightening to contemplate, we had to wait for our flight at Gatwick Airport, and I had worked myself into quite a state, but did my best to hide this anxiety and succeeded to a point, or should I say to a PINT or six!!!!!

We eventually took off, and except for a short period of sheer terror, when the 747 plane climbed and banked, I quite enjoyed the seven hour flight to New Jersey, in Philladelphia, where we landed at about 8pm, we were warned by our courier, that we would experience "jet lag", and that we would probably be "raring to go, sometime after midnight"--she was dead right.

My first thoughts when I stepped out of the "Arrivals lounge" at the airport in America, was how hot the temperature was, which surprised me greatly, as I expected it to be like the weather in Britain, and certainly not so hot, we were taken by coach to our hotel, the first of seven we would be using during our tour, and after checking into our really impressive hotel room, I did my usual reccy' of the apartment, which was well up to what I'd been told to expect, --king sized bed and all!!---Jeannette decided that she would freshen up by taking a shower "en suite", and proceeded to do just that, when suddenly I heard a loud scream, she had slipped on the wet floor tiles, fallen and bumped her head, ----then I discovered that for some reason she had locked the adjoining door, and for some minutes, which seemed like an eternity, the air was filled with Jeannette crying hysterically on one side of the locked door, and me panicking and yelling "blue murder", telling her to unlock the damn thing----on the other!!

My spirits plummeted, when she eventually opened the door, and I saw the injury she had sustained, to the back of her head, --- I had visions of her being laid up in hospital, and our holiday being seriously interrupted, or ruined--- the fact that we were well covered by insurance just never entered my head, and all kinds of scenarios went through my mind, but luckily, Jeannette took control of the situation, even though she must have been feeling dreadful, because she had an awful cut over two inches long, on the back of her head. She went to the Hotel medical officer, who dressed the injury, but Jeannette had a thumping headache for days afterwards.

It transpired that our courier was right, we were awake, and eager to get going at about 2.30 am, and we decided to explore the neighbourhood, found an all night diner, where we sat down to eat a full English breakfast, American style with huge portions --------"Lovely grub"!!!

Whilst making the initial travel arrangements, prior to our trip, I never having been abroad, had been making lots of enquiries, to try to ascertain, roughly how much cash we would need to take with us for spending, and other requirements and consequently I had brought about 7500$ worth of travellers cheques, the exchange rate at that time being $1.5 to the£, but by the time we had returned to Britain I had only spent just over the equivalent of £2500, and had plenty left, for what I planned as a return trip the next year, unknown to me then, but daughter Beverley, was to announce that she, and boyfriend Paul, were getting married, but even though my plans had to be changed, this was no great problem, because Paul has turned out to be a great son in law.

I had been warned, not to carry all my cash in one "lot", and had secreted it in various hiding places, in our luggage, hidden in shoes, and rolled up in socks etc, but thankfully it turned out to be a precaution, which wasn't needed, because we had a superb trouble free holiday.

We landed in New Jersey, and stayed in many hotels on a "whistle stop" tour of the southern States, when we visited Philladelphia, Memphis, Houston, Dallas, Alabama, New York, New Orleans, Washington, Forth Worth, Hendersonville, Nashville, and lots of historic sites along the way, too numerous to name, but tops were Elvis's "Graceland Mansion", Hank Williams' Ranch, and FIVE adjoining mansions, built by Conway Twitty, a country-music super-star, for each of his grown up sons and daughters, -- and also Lorretta Lynn's luxury ranch, as well as a day at the N.A.S.A Space centre, in Houston Texas, --- "South Fork Ranch", of TV's "Dallas" fame, we then had a day cruising the Mississippi River, on the "Natches" paddle steamer out of New Orleans.

During our week long stay in Nashville, we were in the audience on TV on "The Bobby Bare Country Cavalcade" as well as the "Saturday night at the Grand Ole Opry" and whilst we were in the city of Dallas we had a barbecue at the legendary "South Fork Ranch" from the TV series "Dallas " where I took the opportunity to dangle my feet in the swimming pool, -- I later had added to my business cards when I was a rep for Total Oil, the following sentence-- "I've dipped my feet in J.R's pool", which was a superb opening gambit, when I visited "cold" customers, trying for sales

We stayed at "The Hall of Fame" hotel, during our stay in Music City, which was the hub of activity with singers and bands who were appearing at the Opry, and the many venues around the city, and surrounding areas, and I met many big named country singers, the main one being a man named Webb Pierce, who was responsible for introducing the pedal steel guitar to the genre, Jeannette and I had a long conversation with him, and took many photos with him, --sadly Webb Pierce died in 1989.

We ended our tour at "The White House", in Washington D.C before spending a day touring New York and returning to New Jersey to get our flight home. We knew we had arrived home when we landed at Gatwick, after waiting for two hours for National Coaches bus to arrive, I asked the driver if I could put our luggage on the vehicle, whereupon he told me in no uncertain terms "to put it where I ******* wanted to, cos he was ******* running a *******hour late, and he was ******* going to have his ********tea!!!, I didn't expect him to say "Have a nice day Y'all"........but I did miss the American peoples, politeness though.

Boarding in New Orleans, July 1985

Chapter Twelve

A "Wrinklie" Recalls

Having provided the reader with an outline of our life, through the early years, and taking good care NOT to place too much strain on my ageing memory, I will now attempt to embellish the account with tales and anecdotes of those distant days, so as the former singer, radio and TV personality, Jimmy Young, would say, "ORFT we jolly well go!!!".

You will, no doubt agree, that nostalgia is a wonderful inexpensive means of enjoying oneself, and can be done without leaving the comfort of ones armchair on cold winter evenings........Yes!..I know there ARE other ways of enjoying oneself, but I've lost the book of instructions!!!

You will remember that my first home was called "Greenfield" which was only a short distance from where Dad was born, at "Little Farm", West Nash, a village just outside Newport in South Wales, where we would visit, eagerly whenever we could. During conversation, Dad would always refer to "Little Farm", as "down home" which, was a whitewashed, stone built farm house, with several buildings nearby, and to reach the front door one would open a tall iron gate, which would close automatically behind you, due to a simply constructed weight mechanism, then having passed through this gate you would pass along a bowery, a trellis type corridor, or archway which was usually covered by climbing flowers, such as roses and honeysuckle.

On entering the front door, you would find yourself in a sort of interior conservatory, which was also used as a cloakroom, the top half of the interior walls being glass, it was possible to look into the large comfortably furnished living room of the house, and invariably the lady of the house, our legendary "Granny" Bassett could be seen inside.--- Me, being both young and small, at that time, this room seemed large and had a number of dark coloured, heavy wooden beams supporting the low ceiling.

In the right hand corner of the room was a small square window, which looked out upon the well maintained back garden, a door led off to the right into a large cool dairy, and in the opposite far corner a door opened to reveal a winding staircase to the bedrooms.

A number of double barrelled shot guns were hung length ways, along the ceiling beams, and a black German Luger pistol, hung on the wall, high up to the right of the mantelpiece over the fire place, during recent research into the Bassett family history, an interesting fact emerged, in that, Dad's brother Frederick who had gained bravery awards in the first World War had in fact, in his wartime capacity as a "sniper" with the South Wales Borderer's regiment had actually taken a pistol from a German soldier, ---Uncle Fred who was mentioned in despatches had been awarded the DCM and Belgian Croix de Guerre, for these actions, written evidence of this fact is on display at the Local Library and also at the Regimental Barracks, Museum in Brecon. Powis .and it is believed, in some quarters of our family, that this was the pistol, in question.

In the hearth were a number of highly polished shell cases, surrounded by a metal fender, which I believe was made of some kind of gun metal, highly polished-- and above the mantel piece hung a large framed mirror, tilted to face the large kitchen table which, when laid for a meal, was indeed a most welcoming site, resplendent with home made pastry and cakes, butter and cheeses, and I remember fondly that when seated at this table, eagerly awaiting "starters orders", we could see a reflection of all these goodies, in the mirror, as well as a reflection of the high chest of drawers, situated behind us on the opposite side of the room to the fire. I never got to visit Granny Bassett's as often as Arthur or David, but at the time when Aunty Nell was living with Granny Bassett, I heard her say, in the next room, ---- "THAT Robert, he'll eat us out of house and home, Mother!!" ---I must admit that she had me "sussed "---I have always been a self confessed glutton, in hindsight I 'spect that is why I never went there as often as the other two!!!

To the left of the fireplace was a long high window, with a window seat, and I recall, even now the metallic sound of the iron gate shutting, and the approaching footsteps on the cobbled path leading to the front door, which would open, and you could see the person who was entering through the glass of the conservatory as they came into the house. When visiting we children were expected to sit quietly, or to go outside and play, which we were always happy to do, because there was a myriad of things to do to keep us occupied at Granny Bassett's

Being very young, I didn't get to visit Granny Bassett's as often as Arthur and David but I recall a raft that they, along with cousins Brian Aplin, and Dennis Fletcher had constructed out of five gallon drums and lashed together with boards, which was tethered on one of the reed lined ponds situated in the area, now known as "Nash Wetlands", of course they were not officially there then, they were just the natural wild areas of land, Remember, this was before the farm had been compulsory purchased, for the purpose of building the giant Uskmouth Power station, they also used to play on a four wheeled pump action propelled bogie, on the rail-track leading to the sea wall, which would travel at a "fair lick", once the handles were used to build up speed.

Cousin Brian passed away fairly recently (this manuscript was started in 1994. Ed) and sadly, not many of the family had seen, or met him in recent years, except perhaps David, as Brian had spent a lot of his working life abroad, as well as making his home base in Middlesborough, but I think this may be an opportune moment for me to put on record, that me and my family will be forever grateful to cousin Brian for providing the wherewithal for us to undertake urgent repairs to our home, At the time, we had no means of getting the work done, and I just didn't know which way to turn, so cousin Brian, your hard earned money was put to good use, and my family and I will be forever grateful. R.I.P.

When leaving Granny's house, another self closing gate to the right, led onto the farm yard, and the outbuildings, and also led to a long lane, where I believe another Aunt lived, however if one chose to return back along the bowery to the front gate, there was a converted railway carriage, which had been converted into a bungalow, and was the home of my late Aunty Nell and Uncle Horace Davies. This dwelling was in pristine condition, because Aunty Nell was a very house-proud lady, in fact during her later years, when she had moved in with her mother, Granny Bassett, after Uncle Horace had died, she would always clean and polish the fire-grate during the early evening, no matter how warm and inviting the fire was, it would always be greatly reduced in the cleaning process.

Outside the front of the house was a rene, with a narrow footbridge leading to a meadow and a footpath to the nearest road, which, if my memory serves me right, would be where the Uskmouth main gates are now. To the left of the house a railway line passed close by, and the engines which used it, terrified me, they seemed so huge, though I did get to ride on the footplate with the driver once or twice along with Arthur and David.

Mam's mother, the venerable Granny Potts, lived at Portskewett Street, off Corporation Road, Newport, her house was the end of terrace, and one of the hazards of visiting this residence were the large number of geese, which used to wander in from the nearby river bank, they would actually chase you, with necks extended and hissing viciously, I don't know what would have happened had they caught us, --thank goodness I could beat them for speed. The house was red-brick built, and was entered through a small wooden gate, into the yard and through the front door on the gable end. On entering the small hallway there were doors at right angles on either side, and a steep stair-case directly in front, through the door to the right was a large room with a high window which looked out onto the street, and this room was at the time the home of Uncle Charlie and Aunty Betty, who later bought their own home in the adjoining Gaskell Street.

The door to the left was to Granny Potts's living room, and similarly to the first room, the first thing to strike one was, the high sash windows and high ceilings, from which were suspended gas lights, with white mantels and the two long chains with which to turn them "on or off"---they used to fascinate me.

On entering Granny's room, one would turn to the right, and the window on ones left would enable one to look out onto a small back yard, in the centre of the room was a small table and chairs, in the left corner of the room, a door led down some steps to the kitchen area, a fireplace was situated on the far wall, and on the right wall a small door led to what I believe was the pantry, I can still "picture" Grancha Potts sitting in the chair to the left of the fire, and Granny Potts sitting on the opposite side of the hearth, there was no such luxury as central heating in the 1940's.

Grancha Potts was a small man, with a bushy moustache and spectacles, who often wore a flat cap but he would often be without his dentures, probably because, in those days, they weren't made to such a high standard as they are now, and were probably uncomfortable to wear. Granny was I believe a bit of a tartar, and though not a big person, she appeared to be, —of course I was only small then, and without being facetious or disrespectful to their memories, I recall a strong likeness to Ena Sharples and Seth Armstrong, both of television "soap" fame.

I stayed with Granny Potts on many occasions and I recall being sent on "errands" to the shops, the nearest being in the front room of a neighbouring house, and I was always puzzled as to whether it was permissible for me to walk in unannounced, or should I first knock, it was after all a private dwelling.

During the years on our travels we lived in many and varied homes, some nice and others not so good, but one of the treats we used to enjoy was, when Dad and Mam would "don" their best clothes, and leave us on our "best behaviour" as they left to go and see about a new job, we would wait in anticipation, for them to return from their "mission". Then we would sit enthralled to hear that our probable new home, "has got a tap", or "there's a shop", or "it's got a bus which runs twice a week, and it's only a ten minute walk to the bus stop", if you can get a lift, and guess what?, "the man said, they'll be putting the 'lectric in just after Christmas !!!! AND, we can have a pigsty, and he's giving us a quart of milk every day!!!".

The reader will appreciate that in those far off days of our child hood, and due to our often remotely situated homes, we cultivated a logic, with the naivete, somewhat akin to TV's "Beverley Hillbilly's", emanating from our lack of contact with the big wide world. But even so, I can honestly say that we never considered ourselves hard done by, because we thought that everybody lived the same way, unless of course you were lucky enough to be "posh".

When we were at "Brook Cottage", I remember one particular "bonfire" night, we did, as usual, have a huge fire, and the "spuds", but rarely any fireworks, because the shops were too far away, -- on this particular night, the fire was really blazing, Dad was keeping it going great!, and to hopefully "kid" our neighbours, that we also had "bangers etc, Dad would shake the embers, to raise large showers of sparks, followed by rapidly banging "hell" out of the galvanised roof of the lean to shed, ---I dont know what it sounded like from a distance, but we were having a great time ....!

So Dad WAS right after all !!!

When we were children being one of a large family of seven youngsters, keeping ourselves occupied and amused was not a problem, even though television had not yet become a mode of home entertainment, and though we did possess a wireless, having no electricity families were forced to find means of keeping kids occupied especially during the long winter and if or when the battery of the aforementioned wireless had gone "flat" or was at the local iron-mongers being recharged, which usually took about forty eight hours.

During these intermissions, we were left to our own devices, though some evenings Dad (David Sydney Bassett) and Mam (Doris May Bassett, nee Potts) would maybe, having a cup of tea, or during supper, which was the norm in the forties and fifties, and often Dad would reminisce about "down home", which was his way of talking about his younger days, and about how his brother, our Uncle Fred Bassett had fought in the great war, of 1914-1918, and had won medals, which included the "croy dee gerr", and though this was something that none of us had any, or very little information about, but was accepted often with a knowing smile, but truth was, we ALL thought we knew better, and that Uncle Fred could not have possibly won the "French medal" anyway. !!

As I have mentioned earlier, with the very big help of my sister Peggy, and her friends, who have the contacts to obtain difficult information, it has been ascertained that Uncle Fred Bassett had indeed fought in the First World War of 1914-1918, as a "sniper" with the 10th Battalion of The South Wales Borderers. At this point, I include a piece from the publication, "The History of The South Wales Borderers" published in 1999, following a First Edition of 1931, printed by The Medici Society, and obtainable from The South Wales Borderers and Monmouthshire RegimentaMuseumum, at The Barracks, Brecon.

In it is an account of the Battalion's action, I quote, "the 10th gave as good as they got, and in the exchanges between snipers and patrols they scored heavily on several occasions. Private Bassett was particularly successful as a sniper, on one occasion when he and three other snipers were watching a hostile post, seven enemy emerged from it, he opened fire bringing the leading man down, and putting the rest to flight, he then rushed to the body and searched it for identifications, getting back safely,

The following page is the actual announcement taken from the archives of the "South Wales Argus", held on microfiche at Newport Library, which was an extract from the London Gazette.

Peggy and I visited the Regimental Museum in 2006 and the following picture is an actual photograph of the medals on prominent display at the Museum and includes the:-

D.C.M...... Distinguished Conduct Medal, Awarded
to 22143 ..Private Bassett, F. Belgian,
CROIX DE GUERRE. Awarded to 22143.. Private Bassett, F.

SO DAD WAS RIGHT AFTER ALL, !!!!

22143 Pte. F Bassett DCM CdeG
10th Bn South Wales Borderers

For conspicuous gallantry and devotion to duty while watching an enemy post with three other snipers. Seven of the enemy armed with bombs emerged from the post, and when the leader made a sign to his men, two of them rushed to his side, the snipers judging they had been observed, fired, and the leader fell dead. The rest ran back, Pte. Bassett, in full view of the enemy, rushed to the body, made a thorough search, seized the revolver from the dead man's hand, and then made a dash for cover midst a

Medals won by Uncle Fred Bassett in 1914-18 War including the Distinguished Conduct Medal and Belgian Croix de Guerre and Commendation

Chapter Thirteen

Schooldays were the happiest..........

As I have documented in earlier chapters, my school-days encompassed a number of schools of varying academic capabilities, culminating in my arrival at my "alma mater" in March 1948, the imposing red-brick building, which was Bassaleg Grammar school situated just outside Newport in South Wales.

One of the most exciting aspects, having taken and passed the "eleven plus" examination, while still only ten years and ten months old, I found to be, the actual receiving of the large brown paper envelope, which contained, amongst other things, the long list of clothing and equipment, which the fledgeling high-school pupil would require, prior to enrollment at the new place of learning. Now to modern day children this would not raise a flicker of interest, but to kids like me, and my brother Arthur earlier, the thought of having a blazer/blue, trousers/ grey flannel, socks grey/pairs two, together with, geometry sets, pencil cases, satchel/leather, pens and pencils, etc, "et al" was something akin to winning the National Lottery, and, although there was actually about the same odds against us ever receiving the contents of the said lists in their entirety, it was the things of which dreams are made of, and kept us in a state of hopeful euphoria for weeks, just reading and re- reading the contents of our brown envelopes.

Arthur had been luckier, in that his "big day" had occurred some four years earlier when he had enrolled at Jones West Mon School, at

Pontypool, and although every effort was made to "rig" him out as per instructions, Dad's wages weren't conducive to either of us being inundated or overwhelmed with the aforementioned articles, though Mam had no doubt searched for what little assistance was available from the authorities in those distant days, ---nevertheless the mere thought of "going" to such a huge establishment was in itself something to relish, or at least we thought so, and to be able to dine there was even better, -- the reader will recall that the facilities at our village schools were in those days, "modest" to say the least.

Bassaleg Grammar school was, to a small boy, a huge place with long corridors, marble floors, extremely high ceilings and tall windows everywhere, and my first classroom was at the very end of one such corridor, where I was enrolled into Form One North, and where I was designated to my own personal desk, in which I would keep all my own personal books and belongings, but some lessons entailed the pupil to collect the required books and equipment from this room, and to proceed to the allotted room for each different subject, for example Geography would mean a journey from Form One North, along the length of the ground floor corridor, up the wide winding staircase along another second floor corridor, to the "Geography room on the upper floor, where we were accosted by the bustling Miss Gwyneth Meara, commonly known as "Ma Meara", who was very like the late Dame Margaret Rutherford, in both stature and demeanour, Incidentally Miss Meara was actually the niece of the building contractor who actually built the school which was opened in September 1935.

Other members of the teaching staff at my new school were "Ted Evans who taught History, P.O.Davies, French master, "Moggie" Morgan, Mathematics, "Percy" Percival, Scripture, "Gillie" Gilford, Sport and Geography, "Carrots" Porter, German, and of course not forgetting "Gaffer" Rhys T, Harry M.A, our revered Headmaster, later to be replaced by "Blinkin" Penry M Rees.

As I have already said, Arthur, who was by now a fully fledged high school pupil, would often regale us with stories of his days at West Mon, He was very adept at mimicry and I was enthralled to listen to his stories, one such example was one about his Music master, who would intone them to "Get, sat down Boy!!", and one of the songs he was taught was, I recall rightly or wrongly, " The Flying Dons", and the verse I remember went as follows:-

> Haul her away boys, Haul her away !!
> Haul to the beat of Tramp, Tramp, Tramp,
> Oh here's the wind to catch The Flying Don, boys,
>   Haul her away, away boys, haul!!.

I've always remembered these words, though Arthur used to emphasise the words with contorted facial expressions, and we his younger siblings would be held spellbound with his tales of "derring do" at West Mon school.

Arthur was to us younger siblings a bit of a trend-setter in as much that he was usually a bit more "street wise" than us, having the opportunity to travel to Pontypool to school, whereas we lived a more restricted and protected lifestyle in the small village, and consequently he didn't seem to place such a high value on personal possessions, like the rest of us, I recall when David and I had new footwear, we walked on the grass verges to prevent our new boots being scuffed by the rough surfaces of the roads, Arthur was very adept at collecting L shaped "rips", and would often come home from school with a tear in the seat of his grey flannel trousers, which always resembled a letter "L, He usually got this from a rough and tumble, or a "kick-about" game of football, which would not make Mam very happy !!!.

On another occasion we were in awe when one of Arthur's school mates became an instant sporting hero, when he actually played for Usk Town football team in a home match, on The Island" along-side such celebrities as Stan York and Spencer Kear, the boys name was a certain

Peter Poole, who I recall had extremely blond hair, I wonder does big brother remember him.

As I have mentioned earlier, I have, during the passing years crossed paths with many former Bassaleg Grammar school pupils, eg, Graham Rees, son of the B.W Rees and son Ltd, company, who I worked for, and with whom I have spent many pleasant evenings with socially, and of course my neighbour Ralph Pearce, with whom I often have quite lengthy chats with----particularly when I am trying to cut my front lawn !!!

I also attended the funerals of Mr Penry M. Rees, our old Headmaster, and Mr Maurice Gilford, our former sports master, and though the old school is a much larger Comprehensive school now, I am proud of the fact that I AM a former pupil of Bassaleg Grammar.School.

Chapter Fourteen

Marriage

In early 1963, I was well into my weekly routine of borrowing money off Mam, going out every night and drinking heavily, going to work to earn money to pay Mam what I owed –on Friday, so that I could borrow money to go out on Saturday and Sunday, drinking and so on and so forth, -- Mam would often put an embargo on further borrowing, ... for an hour or so, then relent, and it was during one of these lulls in my busy "social life", that I was lying on the settee, "resting my eyes", by dozing fitfully, whilst judging the appropriate moment to ask Mam for "some money to go out".......when a knock on the front door, was answered by Mam, who said, "Robert, there's someone at the door for you!!" --it transpired that it was a lad named Alex Morgan, who asked me to join him and some friends for a evening out......."Mam will you lend me..........?

Alex had a date with a young lady named Julia McCarthy, who had a friend who lived near her.............I changed and dressed quickly, and in due course went to the front gate, got into the Ford Cortina car, belonging to Alex, and joined the smart young lady sitting nervously in the back seat, who timidly asked me, "Do you like rock and roll?" ....I had met Jeannette Mary Lynn, who was destined to become " my other half", and to reap the benefit of my intelligence and undoubted charm, to this day May 2nd 2010, and is at this moment, sitting downstairs in the lounge, watching TV, and hopefully shortly, will call me for my tea,

--- Oh yes, we have earlier had a sumptuous lunch at the Cefn Mably Arms and visited the church at Michaelstone-y-Fedw.

The four of us, Alex, Julia, Jeannette and I decided to head to Cardiff, and eventually ended up at an establishment called "The Ocean club", a popular night club, on Rover Way----where we were refused admission!.... so we settled for an evening at the "Airport Inn" close by, where we spent an enjoyable evening. I remember this establishment because of the ultra modern furniture with extremely low seating, in fact when seated in the chairs our knees were level with our chins.......a distinct occasion of beer and "stocking tops", I was happy!!!!

During the ensuing months Jeannette and I went out every night, I would catch a bus to Maesglas, go and call for her, we would have an evening together ending up at Rogerstone---I would then walk her home down through Tredegar Park to her home, then have the dubious pleasure of the long walk back--- alone, ---usually arriving home well after midnight, OH, then it was vital for me to be up sometime close to 5am, in order to catch my lift to the Daries.--During my amble back through Tredegar Park, it always struck me how quiet and eerie it became as I journeyed homewards.

I would leave Jeannette's home and head to the park gates, and make my way towards the small hunting gate at the Bassaleg end, near the Tredegar Arms pub, feeling quite relaxed and at peace with the world, behind me vehicles could be heard as they travelled to and from Newport, As I walked away from the street lights and houses, and headed towards the foreboding dark avenue of trees, through which it was necessary for me to walk, —the night seemed to suddenly turn cold, dark and still, I looked back toward the main road, and there suddenly seemed to be----no vehicles or signs of life......I would hurry to the top of Forge Lane and rejoin the road, and head down over the river bridge to Pye Corner, and onwards to High Cross lane, which in those days was dark and narrow, not like it is now, all wide and well lit.

I never ever had a door key, Mam would always wait for each one of us to come home, and I would eventually arrive home and descend the steep steps of 17 Hillside Crescent Rogerstone, and knock.............by this time I was usually half asleep, also still half drunk, and my solution to these problems, were to stand close to the door, and lean my head lightly against the cold glass panels in the front door, carefully waiting to see the blurred outline of Mam's white "nightie" as she slowly descended the stairs, ...as she approached the front door, I would draw myself upright to an inebriated lurch, and endeavour to appear casually indifferent, ...as any self respecting lad should.............Mam would call "Who is it?"....... "Me Mamma", !!!........she would then open the door, with the words "You are going to kill yourself in that lorry, if you don't start coming home earlier, Robert!".........I would respond in a mumble "Oh, I'm not tired !!" as I half stumbled and sometimes fell into the bedroom and onto the bed, often waking brother Arthur, who also needed to be up very early, next day, and with whom I shared the bed.

Next morning, which was only a couple of hours later, I would be completely SHATTERED !!!!---and often missed my lift to work, but the next night would be a repeat of this scenario, we went out every night and enjoyed each others company so much that one night whilst walking up through the avenue of trees, mentioned earlier, I suggested that it might be a "good idea", to get married, ...Jeannette nearly "fell over", with shock !!, but eventually we decided to do just that, and arrangements were set in motion, and we were married on October 26th 1963, at St David's Roman Catholic Church at Maesglas in Newport.

As was due my usual meticulous planning, we "had nothing", and as a wedding present, Dad had given me an envelope, with the warning, "not to lose it, Robert, there's money in it !!"----it actually contained fifteen pounds in notes, which was a lot of money, in those far off days. The wedding went very well, thanks mainly to Jeannette's mother, who had quite a bit of influence in the catering trade, due to her position as the manageress of Newport's Majestic Ballroom, on Stow Hill, in the town, and after spending the night at Jeannette's home, we left to catch a double-decker Western Welsh bus to go to Porthcawl, where we had the use of a six berth caravan for our weeks honeymoon.

When we arrived at the caravan park, which being October was officially closed for the season, Jeannette and I spent hours in the dark wind-swept rainy late afternoon, traipsing up and down the avenues of deserted caravans, searching for the one we were to occupy.-- After some hours of sporadic bickering, over the correct instructions, for the name, row number etc, we eventually stumbled across the one, we had been searching for, and were only too glad to crawl into bed, cold wet, irritable and completely worn out !!!............

Early the following morning we were woken up, by a loud knocking on the door of the caravan, so I got up, dressed hurriedly, and opened the door, to be greeted by a stranger, who informed me that we MUST vacate the caravan, as he had instructions to tow it away with the Land Rover he was driving !!-----We were stunned, and the next half an hour or so was spent with Jeannette and I, firstly trying to remember the name of the lady who had given us the use of the 'van—Jeannette could only remember that "it was Mamma's friend, we always call her Cobbin", to which the man kept saying "I'm sorry, but MY orders, are to take it away, so you'll have to get out"........"But it's our blinkin' honeymoon !!!"....... "I'm sorry I've had my orders"......... In the end we gave up, and turned to go and pack our bags, ...with that the man started to laugh and then told us that it was "all a wind up" that had been arranged by Jeannette's family and friends.

We had been there a couple of days and were having a pleasant time, until one afternoon, a policeman came to our caravan, accompanied by the site warden, and wanted to question me, about "the schoolgirl" I had been seen with in the local club, some nights previously, ---this was NOT a "wind up", someone had reported seeing a "nasty looking character, buying drinks, for a slip of a schoolgirl" in the club, days earlier. We then had to produce documents to prove that we were indeed, who we claimed to be.

Jeannette and I have now been married over forty six years, Mam warned me that "it'll never last", and they say that marriage IS an institution, ---my old headmaster said that I'd end up in an institution !!!!---------Let me out!!!

Having enjoyed our week at Porthcawl, we returned home, and I then sprang the next surprise on Jeannette.......previous to our wedding, I had considered the two alternatives that we had, these were either to rent living accommodation, probably rooms, or to live with relatives, and for various reasons neither seemed very inviting, then I spotted an advert in the local paper, "Luxury Caravan on a private site", and being shrewd and a man of decision, I checked it out and immediately "snapped it up". This caravan was parked in a field about 75 metres from the main farm house, at Court Farm, in Caldicot, about nine miles from Newport and owned by a Mr Arthur Jones the farmer.

They already had one tenant, who rented part of the farm house, his name was Brian Price, who at the time was the captain of the Welsh rugby union team, a "British Lion", and a teacher at the large Caldicot Comprehensive school, close by.

I had in the meantime bought a Ford 10 van, which was hand painted, light blue, and was NOT a vehicle likely to impress a newly married young lady, with the prospects of living in a caravan in a field far away from her home environment............it had cost the princely sum of £15 pounds, and also had one or two other unfashionable features----- the two side doors on the driver and passenger sides were kept closed by a length of rope tied from one side to the other, secured after both occupants were seated . Yes, it was strange, but we soon got used to this rope passing chest height from one side to the other in front of us.

The rear doors were secured in a similar fashion, but outside across the back of the van---I should at this juncture perhaps, point out that these were not just ANY old pieces of rope, but specially purchased for the purpose, --------I do like things to be well presented!!.

I bought the vehicle from a friend, who told me that he would let me have the necessary documentation at a later date, after he had sorted out a few minor details. It transpired that our newly acquired vehicle, was actually the bodywork of one old vehicle, welded precariously onto the chassis of another one, and I, not having much interest in technical things, accepted his explanation, because after all, he seemed like "a nice bloke", AND there was still eleven days tax on the vehicle!!

Anyway, I collected the van, and drove to pick up Jeannette, who was waiting at her mothers home, , she still didn't know about our new home, I wanted to give her a nice surprise, !!---I collected her, and we proceeded to make our way out into the country towards Chepstow, she was becoming more and more concerned, as darkness fell and the winter evening closed in, as it got steadily colder and less comfortable in our vehicle, ----it is early November, and eventually we arrived at our destination and I introduce Jeannette, my new wife, to Mrs Arthur Jones, who had a personality akin to TV's Ena Sharples, who gave us the key to our new home, without ceremony, closed the door and left us to find our way to it-----in the dark!!!

We stumbled from the farmhouse, through the rickety field gate, it was raining and wet underfoot, --Jeannette was having difficulty walking in her smart high heeled shoes, and as we made our way slowly up the inclined grass field, I had to admit the "luxury caravan" did look rather uninviting in the murky evening gloom, by this time, Jeannette was getting more and more concerned about the many noises which emanated from the surrounding fields and hedgerows, which hadn't worried me a bit, having experienced like conditions at many of our earlier homes, and I think it became rather obvious that Jeannette was far from happy, and when I opened the door to our caravan and we entered our "new home", she immediately demanded a "swift" return to Newport, with utterances of a "flaming divorce"---------the following days were not much better, but I eventually managed to get "the wife" to settle into our new surroundings.

The caravan was actually a luxury model, but unfortunately well past it best, and was indeed fully oak-lined, with leaded glass doors on all the cupboards and fittings, Jeannette polished everything----our wedding presents were fully laid out, with fruit bowls and cut glass ornaments, and it really DID look lovely, unfortunately on the fourth day it RAINED---inside our beautiful home water dripped everywhere !!!----Jeannette had to reposition all the glass ware to catch the offending water., but then we discovered that water was also seeping down the inside walls and as a result the seats/ beds .on either side were developing mildew underneath, so each dry day Jeannette would take all the cushions etc and clothes outside onto the grass to dry, and air

Our only heat supply was a two barred electric fire, and perhaps at this juncture I should point out that I had made enquiries and discovered that electricity which is sub- let through a second meter on a system, ie from the main supply at the farm house, to us in the van, could legally be set at whatever cost the owner decided to put on it, and our electric fire on ONE bar would last exactly seventeen minutes for one shilling (ten pence in decimal currency)---this may not seem expensive now, but at that time I was earning somewhere between £9 and £13 per week as a lorry driver which included overtime.

Anyway, in my infinite wisdom, I decided that this was a little unfair, and I looked to try to find a solution, and after studying the meter in our chilly abode, I noticed that there was NO official seal on the aforesaid meter, neither could I find any apparent mains switch, which meant that I could not turn off the power to enable me to inspect the device more closely.

One morning days later, after much thought, I removed the black outer casing, by undoing the screws, and, shaking like a leaf, I nervously and carefully inserted a shilling coin into the aperture provided for that purpose, and placing my other hand, where the money box would have been, caught it as it dropped, ---the reader will appreciate my nervousness, because the power WAS still ON, and don't forget electricity is OK so long as it doesn't hit you!!! I repeated the process many times, and we were lovely and warm over the ensuing weeks, I was elated, but I also realised that I had to make sure that the coin-box would contain an apparent acceptable amount in it when our landlady eventually arrived to empty it. One morning weeks later she arrived to do just that, and checking the contents she commented that there seemed to be less than usual, which I hopefully justified by saying that we had of late retired to bed much earlier, due to the extra work I had to do, and the tiredness factor as a result.

She went away, apparently satisfied with this explanation, but some time later "out of the blue" early one morning we were woken by a loud knocking on the door, --it was Mrs Jones, our landlady, calling out that she had come to empty the meter, it was only a little after 7am, so I guessed that something was amiss, but I had already foreseen something like this happening and had recently put fourteen shilling pieces into the meter box, though there should have been closer to £3 in there by now, and "thinking on my feet" I remarked that I had noticed that the silver wheel that I noticeable in most meters, was often still, --- hopefully making her think that there may be a defective part in the device----- --she obviously half believed me, because, she had the meter removed, and we came to an arrangement for me to pay what I considered a much fairer amount each week-- and that was the last, we saw of the wretched thing, I think she realised that she had been "ripping us off" very unfairly, so justice prevailed !!!.

Jeannette had by now become much more settled into country life, and we were both trying hard to make the best of living in Caldicot, ---one morning we were woken by the caravan rocking violently !!, now newly weds we were, but I can assure you it wasn't us, !!---I opened the door to discover that the herd of hefty beef cattle were all gathered around our home, and two of them were using our home to scratch an itch, by leaning against the corner and rubbing themselves violently back and forth.

As I said earlier, the caravan was about 75 metres away from the farm house, and the toilet we had to use was about another 25 metres away at the end of the garden path, and consequently each evening would find me taking the "little wife" by the hand, on a late evening stroll, —to the aforementioned toilet, —every "flipping" night, wet or fine, would see us sally forth, into the darkness.!!!

We lived in Caldicot for quite a while, and daughter Beverley Jane, was born at the Lydia Beynon Nursing Home, which is now a greatly enlarged establishment and is the now celebrated Celtic Manor Resort, she occupied the top drawer of the built in chest of drawers, as a crib for the major part of her early life. In 1963 Caldicot was only a small village, and we were very happy living there, , we were known locally as "the young couple from Court Farm", at the local grocery store, where our weekly bill was £4 .10s, which I paid each Friday on my way home from work, until I had a short spell unemployed, —I had settled the outstanding bill, but due to lack of funds, we didn't go into the shop for about three weeks, during which we lived on practically nothing, until one day a person asked us why they hadn't seen us in the shop, we said we were "stocked up", but they obviously guessed why, because a day or so later the owner of the shop filled a large box with groceries, and insisted we accept it "free of charge"------MR ADAMS YOU'LL NEVER KNOW JUST HOW WELCOME THAT GIFT WAS.!!!

I had been out of work due to heavy snow forcing John Laing Construction Ltd, to "lay us off" until it cleared, --- when we started back it was building council houses at Underwood Estate Llanmartin for Magor and St Mellons Urban District Council, and after having words with the Site Manager, he used his influence to obtain a new council house on that estate for me, because I was a "key worker" and we moved into No 1 Elm Close, Underwood Estate, Llanmartin, --I wasn't really a key worker, but he did me a favour to get me a house, which only further validates my claim that its"who you know that counts" always.

We moved into our new home, in my lovely blue van, and though we had literally nothing, Mam gave us an old bed, that she had been given by her neighbour Mrs Maybury, at Hillside Crescent, which was painted a horrible green colour, and actually had the names of their children scratched on the painted headboard, Jeannette's Mam gave us various other bits and pieces, and we had a square table held together by strips of metal, that someone gave us as a house warming present .

Just after we moved in a sharp moving sales-man called and "conned" us into paying nearly £200 for a Seiman's Vacuum cleaner, and Polisher, --the reader will appreciate how ridiculous this was, -- we had a three bedroomed house, a few sticks of furniture, a 6ft by 3ft carpet, and little else, —the house used to echo, echo, ECHO, —but the floors shone like glass, --- Oh, and my van broke down about a mile away, was vandalised, and eventually bought from me for £4 by a passing gypsy.!!!

My parents and parents-in-law, Bob and Doris Bassett and Bernard and
Catherine Lynn at my wedding

My wedding

My wife Jeannette and her father, Bernard Lynn, on our wedding day
26th October, 1963

The author and his wife Jeannette at their wedding day 26th October, 1963

My daughter Beverley

Wedding of daughter Beverley to Paul Sullivan

137

Amy and Nicholas, Grandchildren

Granddaughter Amy Sullivan, aged 17

Wedding of son Steven to Toni Capnos-Taylor

My son Steven, lead singer of vocal duo 'Red Raw'

Son, Steven

The author and his wife Jeannette

Alcan Choir Rogerstone taken 20th December 2010.
Author 5th from right back row

The author's home

Chapter Fifteen

Working my way, ...Right up to date..........

At the time of my wedding to "my significant other half" in 1963, I was employed as a lorry driver by a company named Short Haulage Ltd, working out of their Dock street Depot, in Newport, my boss's name was a Mr Ken Waters who ran a substantial fleet of tipping vehicles of all sizes, which carried materials all over the country, --I loved the job and although there was no Severn Crossings, and only a short stretch of motorway, the M1, had so far been built, I clearly recall the first time I ever drove on a "motorway" which was in 1962.

It was such a "buzz" to go on this new length of carriage-way, and to be told that there was no stopping, NO SPEED LIMIT, and no right turns, was the thing of which dreams are made of, and exhilarating to say the least.

I was travelling from Brighton, heading to a place called Thrapston, near Northampton and took the M1 towards Bedford, not really sure of the correct route, the motorway was very quiet, as I proceeded onwards, when I spotted one of our company's vehicles heading in the opposite direction on the other carriageway, --- it must be remembered that there were much less traffic on the road in those days, AND there were no crash barriers on the side or central reservation either, just a shallow dip with an open drain, which was rather unkempt too, SO taking care, I crossed the central reservation onto the other carriageway and "hared off" in pursuit of the other vehicle.

It transpired that I was right first time, because when I eventually caught up with the other vehicle, driven by a certain Ernie Whileman, from Llanmartin, --- we were both going in the wrong direction.......... The M1 actually opened in 1959 and for the early part wasn't at all congested, and apart from the well known "Preston By-Pass", traffic was confined to "A" or "B" roads, and in order to get from Newport in South Wales to London for example, one had to travel via Chepstow, Gloucester, Oxford, High Wycombe, Slough on the A40 road. There was actually a ferry operating from Beachley, near Chepstow to Aust on the Bristol side, and I used it a couple of times with my lorry, but, because I had the largest of the vehicles on the couple of times that I used the ferry, I was made to board last, and had to stay parked on the round turntable, situated between the two side boarding- ramps in the centre of the craft. All the vehicles had to drive down the concrete slipway to the ferryboat, moored alongside, then judge the rise and fall of the water in order to drive up the ramp onto this turntable, on which, they would then be man- handled round to drive down the short length of the boat and parked.--from memory I would estimate the turntable to be about 10 feet diameter, the ferry wasn't much wider. And I spent a not very pleasant time, sat in the high cab of my vehicle practically looking over the side, as the ferry bobbed about in the choppy water

It was difficult to board or disembark, because the slip-way went right into the water, and depending on the tide one had to judge the swell and it was easier with a larger wheeled vehicles because with small wheeled cars, it was a bit "iffy" and a number of times cars would accidentally "ram" the corner of the ramp as the boat rose quickly on the swell. The craft wasn't very large, and was rounded at each end, and would make good use of the tidal flow, in that it would leave the slipway and head off up stream, then half way across it would let the flow of the tide drift it back to the other side in a sort of arc.

In 1962 a rail strike practically brought the country to a stand still, and it was at that time that Mr Waters, my boss, and Mr Robert Wynn, of the world famous Wynn's Heavy Haulage Company, then formed the Monmouthshire Tippers Association, whose aim was to generate work and safeguard the future of smaller companies. In road haulage, the permissible driving regs' have always been a source of conjecture, —as a driver it is always difficult to convince the bosses that hold ups do occur as a reason for lateness or whatever, and the arrival of the tachograph was a "god-send", an answer to a drivers prayer, --at last, here was something which would bear out the fact that journeys were more than just, "popping here ", or "nipping down there", as I was often cajoled into taking a load here or there late afternoon on many occasions, much to the detriment of my social life!!

An example of the kind of job lorry driving was, in the early days, I left Newport at 10pm one evening, travelling all through the night to Brighton, and unloaded early the next morning, then drove all the way up the M! to Thrapston, near Northampton, re loaded with phurnacite, a type of coal, then I drove all the way back to Uskmouth Power station in Newport, unloaded then went back to the depot in Dock street Newport and "booked off" and went home to bed, having driven and worked over 22hourss non stop, without a break and all for jut over £13 pounds per week including overtime. We did this type of "run", seven times in a fortnight!!!

I left road haulage for a short while for financial reasons and obtained work with John Laing Construction, at Llanmartin, working as a shuttering hand, where they were finishing the 2nd and 3rd phases of Underwood Estate for the Magor and St Mellons U.D.C, and as I have mentioned earlier, the company helped me to obtain our first three bedroomed council house, but I soon had the urge to go back driving and obtained a job with Penhow Quarries Ltd driving a six wheeled tipper, but the wages weren't good, so I then tried a similar job with Thermalite Ltd at Uskmouth, but that was just as bad.

One evening in 1966, I spotted an advert in the South Wales Argus, which stated that "ready mix lorry drivers" were required by F. Bowles and Sons at their Eastern Wharf Depot, in Newport, I applied, and consequently attended an interview. Some days later I answered a knock on our front door and came face to face with a man who was to become a very good friend and work colleague for the next thirty odd years, his name was Frank Young, who informed me that his boss had asked him to tell me that, my job application had been successful, and that they wanted me to start the following Monday.

I had no transport of my own, but Frank offered to let me travel with him, and we agreed to share the cost of the petrol, we duly started to travel together, and really became very good mates, Frank was a lovely man, and a very conscientious worker, and also something of a workaholic, but I can never recall anyone having a bad word to say about him, in all the years we worked together. Although I lived near Frank and his family, wife Brenda, and daughters, Julie and Carol, we only worked together for originally eleven years at F W Bowles and sons, Ltd, as lorry drivers working out of their depots at Newport Cardiff, Merthyr, and Machen, but because at that time the construction industry in South Wales, was really very busy, I got a bit fed up with the long hours interfering with my boxing career, and social life, I decided to change jobs, and subsequently went to work for Unigate Ltd at the Jenkins Street Depot in Newport, , --delivering milk door to door, for about four months, --- which nearly "drove me mad", I hated every minute of my time there!!!---I then got offered a job, driving a petrol tanker for a family owned fuel distribution company, named Collingbourne Fuels Ltd, at Lilleshall street, off Corporation Road in Newport.

This was to turn out to be one of the best moves, that I ever made, I started with the firm in 1978, and loved every minute, driving my tanker, and over the ensuing quarter of a century, I had some marvellous times in the oil industry, as I graduated from being a driver, to Transport Controller with the French Nationally owned Total Oil Company, who had purchased Collingbourne Fuels Ltd, when Mr Jack Collinbourne retired in 1981.

The oil industry is a very fast changing industry, and due to ongoing financial changes such as "dock royalties" ie the cost of storage and throughput etc, Total decided to move their British operations to the North of England, and consequently sold our Depot to Lowes Oil, a Sheffield based company, later to be re-branded as UK Petroleum Ltd, with Terminals in Royal Edward Dock in Avonmouth, as a result of which, we all received a nice "ex gratia", redundancy payouts from Total Oil Ltd and I continued when UK Petroleum took over, but in so doing changed my job to that of Area Sales Representative, and continued successfully until I was offered improved terms to change companies to work for another family owned company, Severn Fuels Ltd of Caldicot near Chepstow, initially as a sales Rep, and then being promoted to the position of Depot and Transport Manager, where I remained until July 4th 1991.

For about a year or so as a tanker driver at Collingbourne Fuels I had kept in touch with Frank Young who had remained at F Bowles Ltd which had "gone public" as British Dredging Ltd, and I had been trying to persuade him to come into the fuel industry, but he had resisted my powers of persuasion until one day he agreed, and we renewed our friendship, this time as tanker drivers, until I sat and passed my Transport Managers Examination at Blackpool College in 1979 and got promoted to the position of Transport Controller with Total Oil (GB)Ltd

Two years or so later I moved to Severn Fuels Ltd as Depot and Transport Manager, although I went there as a Sales Representative initially.

This company which had been started, as a small lubricants company, by a father and son partnership in rented offices etc at the Severn Bridge Industrial Estate at Caldicot, a village near Chepstow in Monmouthshire, trading as Production Lubricants Ltd and was soon to become a well run and established lubricants blending company, with their own registered brand of high quality products, later entering the fuel distribution and sales side of the industry. The Managing Director, father John (R. J) Mould and his son Andrew, (A.G) soon built the company into what has become arguably the top company in the field of fuel and lubricants in the Principality, over the ensuing years, to the position of prominence it now enjoys, .and I like to think that I hopefully played some positive part in that growth.

The company was soon to move from its original leased home, when they had a small fuel storage depot was built on land purchased in the neighbouring village of Ifton, where it became Severn Fuels Ltd, based at the aptly named Ifton Oil depot. I was by this time promoted to the position of Depot and Transport manager, and the company also obtained a small rented premisses in Avonmouth, with staff also based there to cover the West country. The company soon grew and further progress was made when a custom designed, much larger fuel storage supply depot was built, on land at the Progress Industrial Estate at Station Road in the neighbouring village of Rogiet.

I worked here for many years and enjoyed my work very much, being involved in selling and also organising the deliveries and the operating side of transport management, and soon became a "workaholic", practically "living" on the job, I was aftrerall doing the job I always wanted and enjoyed every minute, I was well treated and was given all the "trappings" of my own office, company car etc. Unfortunately my health began to let me down and I developed acute angina.

I had first met a young Andrew Mould when he used to visit Collingbourne Fuels Ltd, later to be changed to Totalheat, a branch of the Total Oil (GB) Ltd, a French company, at Lilleshall Sreet in Newport, he was an enthusiastic young man and who with his father the late Mr R.J Mould had formed their own company Production Lubricants Ltd, which was later to expand into Severn Fuels Ltd as stated earlier, Andrew was a personable young man and told me many years later that his "driving force" was adrenalin, raised by gaining new customers and successful selling........he along with his late father certainly made a success of building what is now one of the most impressive of fuel distribution companies.

My condition caused me quite a bit of discomfort and at the suggestion of Mr Mould I visited my doctor who said that so long as I took my medication regularly he saw no reason for me to stop work, so I continued, but transport is a very stressful business with unexpected hold ups or breakdowns which seemed to occur often at the least convenient moments, and it was during one of these that I made a decision that was to give me many moments of regret—I decided I could not continue and I walked into the main office and informed Mr Mould that I wished to tender my resignation.

I loved selling fuel and lubricating oil, and over the previous years had made lots of friends, and gained many good customers, who I considered as friends, but in the process became something of a workaholic, and it was not unusual to find me in my office on Sundays and Bank Holidays, "honing" some idea or system to a finer degree, or such like, I was "salaried" so obviously I wasn't paid any overtime, but it never worried me because I lived for the job, and loved every second!!

Frank Young died in 1990, and is buried alongside his brother Keith, at the small Chapel at Llanvaches, Charlie Booth my old boxing trainer died in 1988, and is buried in the small village churchyard at Llanmartin, they were some of the nicest people I have ever had the privilege of knowing, I really miss them very much.

I visited Underwood Estate on July 4th 2007 to see how the old place was looking, sadly like many other places many changes have taken place, and though I searched for some time, I couldn't find Charlie's grave, but will try again one day!!

In late 1990, early 1991, whilst working at Severn Fuels, I had been experiencing severe chest pains, and also in my arms, and though I wasn't too concerned it WAS a "blinkin" nuisance, but I found it difficult to get time to see a doctor, as I found it hard to get someone to deputise for me ---"I was part of the furniture", but eventually I began to feel so bad that on one occasion I was taken by one of the office staff, to the local clinic in Caldicot, and THIS forced me to visit my own doctor, who gave me a prescription and told me to go back in a week etc.

Instead of "going sick" as advised, I carried on working with the idea of "working my way through it"-------After-all I did have an oil company to run, didn't I ??.

It is now December 2010 and I am now putting the finishing touches to this biography, I have spoken on the telephone twice to Andrew Mould first, after reading the shocking news of Mr Moulds death in a road accident in Spain about two years ago, following which I put together a short DVD tribute to his father as a mark of my respect to who I still consider to be a superb businessman. I have also heard that a former colleague from those days, Arthur Emberton who was a long time friend and work mate had also passed away

I was invited out to share a coffee with Andrew and the people I knew at Severn Fuels but as yet I haven't enjoyed that experience, time passes and I must get round to it soon.................

Chapter Sixteen

Brothers and Sisters.......

The reader will maybe notice that this manuscript mainly contains tales and anecdotes about myself and two elder brothers, Arthur and David, --Noel was born about two years after me, and had the distinction of being born on Christmas Day, December 25ᵗʰ 1941, but only he can say if that is a good or bad thing from his personal point of view. When we went to school together, I think his first school would have been Caerleon Infants, because I know that I used to worry that the bus might leave without us two, as we "slept" on our camp beds as mentioned in earlier pages, but I dont remember too much about his involvement, that is, until we eventually arrived at Pant Cottage, in Tylla lane, some years later when the four of us, Arthur, David, Noel and I would play football in the fields which surrounded our cottage.

The teams would be Arthur and Noel versus David and I and I think that the reason for this arrangement was probably the age factor, Arthur would have been about 15, Noel about 9=24 years total, David, 13 and me 11=24 years------- I may be wrong, but it seems logical, and over the years it was usually a case of the older sibling leading the younger, and seemed to work well in our case.

When Arthur and David had progressed into working and later into the Forces, Noel and I had to get on with growing up, and at one time I was attending Bassaleg Grammar school whilst Noel was at Pontllanfraith Technical school, I hope these facts are fairly accurate, but those days are in the very distant past, and are distant memories now, Noel did however take and pass his apprenticeship and became a qualified "Fitter and Turner"-----whatever that entails, and I think also that David had served an apprenticeship with W.E King the Joiners, a Newport company, and of course there came a time, when Dad, Arthur, David, Noel and I were all employed by Cambrian United dairies, at the Marshfield Depot situated halfway between Newport and Cardiff.

I believe I was the first to leave "the Dairies" permanently, to pursue a driving career with a number of companies, though both Arthur and I left the Dairies only to return on a number of occasions to work for the firm, , I believe Arthur left to go to "Horrells Dairies" in Rumney as well as "Mothers Pride Bakery" also in Rumney only to return to C.U.D. I of course had a couple of "twoing and froing" with B.W Rees and son Ltd, and later a short spell at Unigate Ltd Jenkins street, Newport. Dad and David were the next to leave the Dairy, after an altercation with the then Manager, one Brynmor Lewis, Noel continued at the Dairy for a good number of years as a fitter, but I believe he then moved to Lovells Ltd at their Leaway Estate factory in Newport until his eventual retirement.

Arthur remained at the Dairies right up to his eventual retirement, although he like David and Myself was originally a farm worker, as was Dad, Arthur then worked for a bakery and another smaller dairy in Rumney on the outskirts of Cardiff, until finally finding his niche at Marshfield, initially being taken on as a dairy labourer, like David and I all those years ago, he worked his way "through the ranks", as it were to eventually fill the position of Dairy Manager at the Marshfield plant, later to become "Dairy Crest Ltd", and even after his retirement I believe he is often called upon in a consultative capacity, He has for a long time lived in close proximity to his former workplace although it has now been turned into an estate of rather select domestic dwellings

Arthur's wife Verlie, was also employed at Marshfield, as office staff, but I believe she then went to work for Tesco's in their general accounts department in Cardiff---Jeannette also worked in Tesco's Accounts in

Cardiff, some years earlier, before she eventually reached retirement whilst employed by the local Authority in Newport as a Leisure attendant at Glebelands, off Caerleon Road in Newport, where she led an active part on the Ladies Bowls scene, and had gained representative honours for Monmouthshire Ladies, a well as being the Team Captain, and Secretary at various times, unfortunately she was diagnosed with ovarian cancer in September 2008 which necessitated in a serious operation and many visits to many different hospitals over the intervening months, she is however progressing satisfactorily at the present moment, May 12th 2010.

David and Mam bought a comfortable Flat on Bryngwyn Road Newport in Holmevalley House, where they lived comfortably for a number of years until Mam died in 2001, he now lives alone there, and does a lot of walking and is out and about most every day. He did have part time employment until quite recently.

Noel has a family, wife Christine, and daughters Helen and Joanne, and son Peter, Joanne the youngest had a terrific 21st Birthday party on April 21st 2004 at the Rogerstone social club, which we attended and had a great time, Noel and Christine live at High Cross estate in Rogerstone. And Helen, who's wedding Jeannette and I attended also lives close by, Peter lives with his wife Ruth and his family in Newport.

My sister Carol who is now separated from her husband used to live in Rogerstone but now lives in Newport, and daughter Claire who's wedding we also attended I believe lives in the Risca/ Cross Keys area, son Herbie and partner also live in that area too, Carol who is known by all our family as "Chick" also has a number of grand children.

Wendy, my other sister and husband Richard Plaisted live in Helsby an area of Cheshire with their family of Elizabeth and Christopher who by the time this manuscript gets put into print will probably have families of their own, I think it's fair to say that Wendy was the "apple of Dad's eye", possibly because that like myself she also had serious health problems as a child, and she was, after all the first daughter after four boys for Mam and Dad, so I guess they were delighted and relieved to see her!!.

Sister Margarette, or as she is known to the family, "Peggy", used to be something of a mirror image of myself when she was younger, all teeth, fair hair, and a "daft" sense of humour, but luckily for her she grew out of it, and now, like myself, has matured into a fiendishly attractive elderly person!!! Husband Alan, who I think was a dolphin in an earlier life, is addicted to water and swimming!!!---live in Twyford near Reading, their family daughter Emma, recently married fiancé Bryn at the rather smart "Monkey Island Hotel" at Bray on the Thames, where we all enjoyed a lovely weekend at what was a terrific occasion, on September 25th 2004—Emma is the image of her Mum, and new husband Bryn is rather a "presentable young dude" and I believe that they have recently moved into their new home--------Good Luck to you both!!!

Peggy's other two offspring, Andrew and Sophie, --Mam always said she cheated at Monopoly, are both making good progress in their chosen career paths.

Arthur and Verlie, now both retired and the whole family, with the exception of sister Wendy, who was unable to attend, accepted Mandy's invitation and enjoyed a tremendous evening at Castleton Masonic Hall on December 19th 2004 for a surprise celebration of Arthur's 70th birthday, which actually fell on December 20th---a terrific night, —son Julian is "mine host" at a pub in the Swindon area and has two smashing children, Samuel and Joseph, while Mandy and her family live in Yorkshire and also have two gorgeous "little 'uns", Phoebe and Alice, all of whom we met at the party

Although they are both retired Arthur and Verlie work twice as hard and are usually to be found "en route" to somewhere or other, either to help Julian, "behind the bar", or to visit Mandy, and probably to spoil the children "something rotten" in so doing.

Personally speaking, I think we have a great family, and though most of them fight shy of ever expressing open emotion, I've no doubt that should the need ever arise, no would be "left wanting"

Family celebration of Mother's 90th birthday, 21st April 1999 at Castleton

Wedding of my younger sister Wendy to Richard Plaisted

Wedding of younger sister Carol to Richard Gough

Nephews and nieces at Twyford

Nephews and nieces at Church Street Rogerstone (Christopher and Elizabeth Plaisted, Richard Gough, Emma Sarsby holding Andrew Benest and Claire Gough)

Wedding of niece Emma Sarsby to Bryn Shaffner

Wedding of niece Elizabeth Plaisted to Lawrence Ritchie

Nephew Andrew Benest climbing in the Swiss Alps. The two peaks in the background are Mont Blanc (15632 ft) and the Weisshorn (14644 ft). The photo was taken after a hard day's climbing.

Niece Sophie Benest, all dressed up and getting in the mood to go to Henley Regatta.

Nephew and niece Peter and Helen Bassett

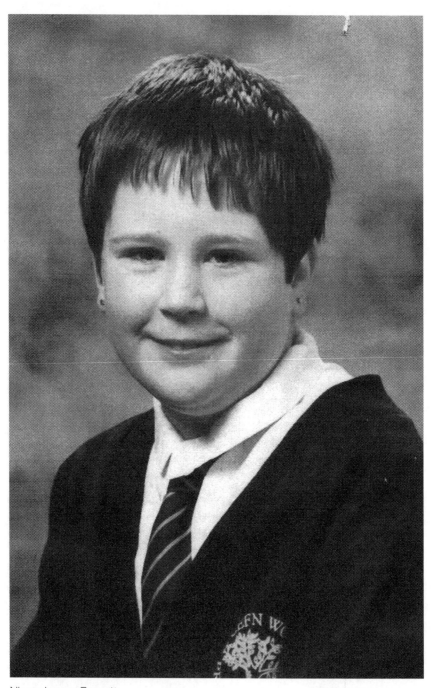

Niece Joanne Bassett

Great-nephew Lucas Shaffner, causing mischief on his first birthday

Chapter Seventeen

Living la vida loca!!!.......We've been together now for forty years......!!!

I have been so busy, trying to remember the events and happenings over the past half century or more, that I almost forgot to do what is the final chapter of this manuscript, ---I mean my lifetime spent with the "slip of a schoolgirl" that I was spotted with, in a pub in Porthcawl, back in 1963, Mam said it wouldn't last, but we are still together, well into the 47th year of our marriage, so either Jeannette is desperate, or I'm daft, or maybe.........

We have had some very hard and difficult times, as no doubt most couples do, and there have been times when Jeannette has performed miracles, to get things sorted, after I have been clever enough to "dig us" into a hole, and as I type I'm thinking of one occasion back in 1980's, when I earned the wrath of our bank manager at Nat West Bank, by casually trebling the amount of the overdraft, that I had been allowed---it would have been a lot more, but I had allowed myself to run out of cheques !!---when I applied for a new book, he spotted my "deliberate mistake".......and requested an interview with me.....at my earliest convenience.....OR ELSE!!!

On July 4th 1991, my medically enforced retirement day.....which incidentally Americans call Independence Day, —I decided that I would hand over the "financial reins" to the "little woman"....or did she decide??....anyway, that's when I was allocated my weekly allowance of

£7 per week, and I have stuck rigidly to the agreement, index linked of course, or so Jeannette says, ...I'm still only getting £15 even now, nineteen years later!!

But seriously though, there have been times when I have had reason to thank Jeannette for so much, and the example that I have just quoted, while it may sound a bit frivolous, WAS an episode which actually happened, when my employment with Severn Fuels Ltd came to a premature end, voluntarily I must add, prior to my being classed as unfit to work, due to health problems, and I went from a well paid job, with a company car, expense account, and all the trimmings, down to £36 per week sick pay, no car, and even worse, no future prospects--------I really did contemplate suicide !!!!!

Jeannette managed to find me a car for £100, and made numerous visits to our Bank Manager to sort out ways to unravel the mess that I had landed us in, then after many difficult years, when she worked at a job which wasn't the easiest, or the most pleasant, that she could have chosen.....I had the marvellous privilege of making the FINAL payment to the Halifax Building Society, to complete our mortgage, actually one month ahead of schedule---I felt like a KING that day in February 2002.-----THE HOUSE WAS PAID FOR.

Jeannette has continued to slave at Glebelands for Newport Borough Council as a leisure attendant, right up to her retirement in 2003, and I had the benefit of her hard work, inasmuch, that I always had a car to "float around" in, and anything else that I needed or wanted, though for my part, I have always tried to make things easier for her, so that she didn't have too much to do when she came home from work in the evenings, though to be honest, she didn't have to do much to persuade me to LET her do all the cooking each day, because she IS a superb cook, and I am good at tasting and eating food.......Aunty Nell said I'd eat them out of house and home !!!......it has been my forte for years.!!!

I do all the preparation of the vegetables, potatoes, carrots etc........so she really ONLY has to cook them...........I'm good like that!!

Seriously though, I would like to pay a sincere tribute to Jeannette, for her love and support since our wedding at St David's R.C Church, Maesglas Newport on Saturday October 26th 1963, for all the happy times and the unwavering support through many hard and often difficult times,

I OWE HER EVERYTHING !!!

Well dear reader, here I am in July 2007, working my socks off, trying to bring this epic set of memoirs to a definite close, once and for all!!

Beverley, and husband Paul live close by with daughter Amy and son Nicholas, known affectionately as "My young THUG", and a couple of doors down their street lives Beverley's brother Steven who is married to Toni, with her children from her first marriage Aimee and James. ---Steven does a lot of semi professional singing with his mate Colin Marsh, around the clubs under the stage name, of "Red Raw". They are quite popular and in demand, though Steven has done many solo dates, and I had the pleasure of accompanying him to a number of venues, and after hectic travelling we often never got to bed until the early hours of the following morning.

To daughter Beverley, let me say that each time I see her I think she's beautiful and a credit to her Mother.

To Nicholas, he is still my "little thug", but absolutely brilliant with his cards tricks.

To son in law Paul, a smashing bloke and a good soccer player.

To son Steven, I'm pleased to see he has found himself a lovely wife, and a great family, in Aimee and James, and I love seeing "Red Raw" too -------ROCK ON!!!

Country Rock, Poems and Pints.

Throughout my life I have enjoyed many differing tastes in music, as mentioned in earlier chapters, and this interspersed with my burgeoning career as a ** "sot" of some renown, throughout the Western Valleys, coupled with my lengthening association with the earlier mentioned "Rogie Boys" and having heard a recording of a monologue entitled "Big Bad John", by a country singer named Jimmy Dean, being always game for a laugh, I often used to perform impromptu songs at the various pubs and clubs that we frequented in those far off days.

Realising that the way to get a good response from an audience was to somehow involve them, so I wrote and used to perform a piece called "The Rogerstone Boys" to the tune of "Sixteen Tons" a song made famous by the late Tennessee Ernie Ford, and over the ensuing years this little number earned me many a "beer check",

I've always been interested in lyrics and verse, but listening to a radio interview with the late great Johnny Cash gave me the "push" to have a go at writing them myself, when he mentioned that he was mystified why British artistes always sang about American events etc, when there are lots of similar things in British history to sing about---shortly after this the Aberfan Disaster occurred, and in the following pages you will find my tribute to those poor kids, as well as a number of other events which followed over the ensuing years.

In 1973 I met a professional country singer from the West Country, who performed under the name of "Ramblin' Mal Daron", when I was involved in running a country music venue at the Roundabout Pub on Nash Road, Newport which was called "The Circle M Country Music Club" he arranged and recorded two of my songs, —I had them both on cassette tapes, which I gave to friends, but I guess they are long gone now, --unfortunately I have lost contact with Mal Daron too.

He was however a fine artist, a brilliant yodeller and a superb whistler and instrumentalist, and was the resident artist and compere at our club which ran for a number of years.

The two songs he arranged and recorded were "The Price of Comfort" and "That's Country", but there are other examples of my work in this manuscript which I hope you enjoy also.

NB:- ** A "sot" :- defined in the Oxford English Dictionary as---A person who enjoys liberal quantities of wine etc.......an habitual tippler !!!.......Yeah, that's me, all-right !!

"The Rogerstone Boys".

Now this here's the story of the Rogerstone Boys,
When we're on a spree we make one hell of a noise,
Singing rock'n'roll, and rhythm 'n' blues
With Des Andrews on the drums.
I'm strutting "Blue Suede Shoes",

Chorus . . . . Get 'em off, What a noise!
           It's ole Des Andrews and the Rogerstone Boys.

Old Ron Theobald is kinda narrow and lean,
With a voice like a poor man's Terry Dene,
But when he gets on stage, Man!, What a sight!!
In his cowboy suit singing, "Are you lonesome
tonight?",

Chorus . . . . Where' the pain, What a noise
           It' ole Ron Theobald and the Rogerstone Boys.

Dud Jones, a swinging guy, I know none cooler,
With a way out style of singing "Be Bop A Lula",
And for a beer check, worth just two and a tanner
Mr Elwyn Phillips would "murder Diana ",

Chorus . . . . That aint singing, It's just a noise,
           Dud Jones and Elwyn Phillips and the Rogerstone
           Boys,

Me and Malcolm Satherley are pretty big mates,
Both long and tall, with feet like plates,

We've got the build to make good coppers,
But they wont take Malcolm, he's got false choppers.

Chorus . . . . Get off this stage, stop that noise,
It's Malcolm Satherley and the Rogerstone Boys.

Now the last of our band is Keith William Lee,
He's got the build, lady rabbits love to see,
But though he's short and fat, and built all wrong,
I have to admit, he can sing a good song.

Chorus . . . . Does he hell, it's just a noise,
It's Keith William Lee and the Rogerstone Boys

Now I've taken the mickey, I guess that's true,
But there's one more thing I want to say to you
We may act crazy, that may well be so
But we're the best rock'n'rollers in the valley's you
know.

Chorus . . . . So clap your hands, make lots of noise !!!
I'm Bert Bassett......We're The Rogerstone Boys !!

That's Country, Man!!

Big John Cash sings song of Folsom Prison
Merle Haggard digs Muskogie
Ole Gene Autry, He just urges cattle
"Git along thar little dogie"

George Jones, loves Dolly Parton,
Bill Monroe he's the blue grass king,
They all love the Grand Ole Opry,
Country songs are what they sing.

Hank Williams and Jim Reeves,
Both sad to say, "passed on",
They're till country music legends
Glad to know that genius, lives on.

Songs of love and heartbreak,
Green fields, Blue skies up above,
Sung for us by country music people,
In the style that we all love.

YEP !! …... That, s Country, … Man!!

1970

My Night.

I stand in my corner and wait for the bell.
Hoping and praying, Lord let me do well
My mouth is so dry, I'm really up tight,
February 12th 1970, Tonight is my night.

A phone call on Sunday, right out of the blue,
Said "Step forward Robert, your country needs you",
Now I'm walking on air, as if in a dream,
As light-heavyweight, in the Welsh Boxing team.

Overweight at the weigh in, but I MUST box for Wales,
Hard work-outs, Hot steam rooms,
Then it's back on the scales,
Three times, but I've made it...Just two hours left, to rest
Completely shattered, right now..but I WILL do my best.

The bell for Round one, we're starting to move,
Straight left, Hook, then Jab, I'm right in the groove,
But then I got careless, the crowd with a roar,
Told me the bad news, -Bob you're on the floor!

I climbed up at eight, he moved in for the kill,
But I made up with effort, what I lacked in skill,
And all through the second, and right through Round Three,
That Dutchman tossed leather, It landed on me.

We gave it "our all", right up to the bell,

The crowd roared, I knew, HE had let me do well,

And though years may pass by, my hair's turning white,

February 12th 1970, will always be,

My Night !!!

1975

An Old Man's dream.

I'm sat at home dozing, half sleeping
Nothing much to do, nowhere to go,
Was that the bell? No I must have dreamt it,
But wait, !! There it goes again, - the phone !!
I pick it up—Hello Bob—It's Charlie.

They want you at Merthyr, next week, !
I must be dreaming..Who?..Wales A.B.A,
You're picked to meet the "Dutch",
On Thursday.....What weight?......Heavy?
No Light-Heavyweight!!! YOU, must be dreaming!!!

I'm now a heavyweight!!.....You're joking !!
No...it's true....Too Heavy!!....What's eight pounds?
Still four days to go.....eat less!!...I guess,
I might never get another chance...I'll try!!
Who am I fighting...a novice??.....Great!!

Black coffee, by the gallon, but NO food!!
But I'll do it........here's the coach, ...I'm dreaming !!
Welsh Officials, Stars !! and ME !! to weigh..
Oh Hell, !! two pounds too heavy !!......now what??
Lose the weight !!.....two hours, ??...then come back !!

Forfeit the fight....two hours.....You just wait !!
Skipping.....Sweating !........Gasping...one last try !!
Get on the scales....I'm shattered !!
You're on the mark !!! get changed.....Yippee !!
I've done it !!!!!now just let me sit and rest !!!

I'm in the ring, for WALES !!!, I'm dreaming !!!
Here's the Mayor !!...I'll wake up soon......no doubt !!
I'll sit and wait my turn, ...Hell !!, here we go!!
The Bell !! he's coming at me !!......Move,
Around the ring...He's blinkin' good !!.....take that!!

What was that....where am I ?? on the floor!!!
I climb up at "eight".......keep moving!!
Calm down Bob!!...use your left !...the bell!!
Sit down, these gloves are heavy !!!...rest!!
Hello Charlie..have a drink......must rest !!

Round Two......that's better !!......I hit him !!
Go forward Bob.....BBC, Red light .....I'm on TV,
Keep moving...Hell these gloves ARE heavy,
There's the bell....Thank God.....sit down !!

Harry Carpenter ??..Round three, I'm tired!!
Keep moving...Great I caught him.. then !!
"Don't Hold".....OK mate !!......I'm tired !!
Not long to go, I hope !!.......Ring that bell !!
"Well Done Bob !!".....sit down.. Hello Charlie !!

We're in the centre of the ring....it's bloody hot !!
The crowd are clapping....Well done ..Charlie !!
I've lost but no disgrace, ...He's good!!
Olympic Games, third place.......He did ??
YOU fought Jim Verstappen !!......I did ??
I WASN'T DREAMING THEN ???

<u>2008</u>

Aberdare.

I'm off to Aberdare, how I hate the calls up there,
Them hills are "hairy", Mr Collingbourne you know!,
The roads are narrow, mountains high
I get so "up tight", I could cry!
Oh, How I wish that you would tell me
"Bob don't go", !!

With a heart full of remorse,
Set my lorry on it course,
Hit the road, Bye Bye Cheeky, ORFT we go!!
From Crumlin to Ebbw Vale,
There's a queue upon my tail,
And I wouldn't be surprised if it don't snow!!.

I sing, I think, I hum a tune !!,
My watch shows, it's half past noon,
Find a lay-by, pull up Stirling!!
Have your scoff !!
Hell it's snowing, Roll 'em son,
One call left, the load is done,
Then it's "hot foot" down to Anne's,
She'll get em off !

Hammer all the way to Risca
Missed a 'decker by a whisker!
Hell, ! His cars there,
Thought she said "He's two till ten"
Never mind son, it's too bad
Belt on down see Mam and Dad,

Have a double helping,
When you call again.

George street bridge, what a night!
Bowketts Depot, on the right,
And I'm last again tonight
But I don't care
It was killer of a run,
But next time I'll have my fun,
When I'm coming home
From good old Aberdare.

Folks, as you know from time to time,
I tend to burst forth into rhyme,
Things I type, really just aint right
Because it's all a load of nonsense
Aided by "poetic licence"
That' MY Story
If I'm last again tonight.

1981.

The Ballad of Locherbie.

A Seven forty seven came crashing to the ground,
Scenes of death and devastation
Scattered miles around,
The plane it didn't fail, No sign of pilot error,
It was evil caused by men, Hell bent on causing terror,
Rows of shattered houses, pain and death so plain to see,
Caused by terrorist, to the town of Locherbie.

It had no rhyme nor reason,
The culprits showed no gain,
The night that shattered Jumbo descended in the rain
The engines didn't fail, a bomb blew them away,
And spread both grief and suffering
On Locherbie that day
But evil must NOT win, right must show the way,
And God will ask the questions for this crime,
Come Judgement Day.

So people say a prayer, Sinners mark me well !!,
For what you did to Locherbie,
MAY YOU ROT AND BURN IN HELL !!

1983.

The Moorgate Train that died

They rode the train to Moorgate,
Under London town,
As it hurtled to the station,
Not even slowing down,
It should have braked and halted,
Gradually the experts said,
But it thundered to oblivion
Leaving all those people, ... Dead !!

The driver's face wash ashen,
His eyes were open wide,
As it hurtled to the station,
On it's crazy headlong ride,
The brakes they didn't fail,
Nothing seemed to have gone wrong,
For Moorgate, spell disaster,
Destination, Speed, Headlong !!,

Coach loads full of normal people
Ordinary hope and fears,
Left a host of grieving relatives,
Crying bitter tears,
Why did it have to happen?
Tear stained faces cried,
Only God would know the answer,
For the Moorgate train that died.

1988

185

Joey's Song

We hit the road to London,
That warm September day,
To see a guy called Cooper
Thumped by Joe, from Tiger Bay.

We'd packed our coach with booze,
Card games were rampant now,
We passed through Reading, all half cut,
Had lunch, then on to Slough.
Cooper, He stood NO chance,
Pal Joe, would murder him
Joe Erskine, was pure magic
Another "Peerless Jim", (Driscoll)

Preliminaries were over,
Joe was doing fine,
A clash of heads, Joe's eye is cut !
Ref' stopped the fight, Round Nine !,

Cooper jut got lucky,
Welsh men cried bitter tears,
We'd lost our Champion heavyweight,
We'd had for three short years.

But Welshmen are born fighters
Courage an in-born thing,
And when we find our next Champ',
This land of song, will sing !!.

1989.

186

A Countryman's Dream

A seven forty seven out of Gatwick
That day July 12 '85.
Up up and away, to the US of A
From then on, my dreams came alive.

The airport, New Jersey, we touched down,
My heart was starting to sing,
Rode a Greyhound to Memphis
And wandered round "Graceland",
The home of Elvis, "The King".

Way on down, to Houston and Dallas,
To "South Fork", JR wasn't home,
But the evening was great,
Country music, till late,
With Jerry Lee, at the vast Astradome.

We travelled at dawn into Nashville
A "dream" for fellows like me,
At the Opry, that night,
Hank Snow, Faron Young,
Charlie Pride, and The Tennessee Three.

For days we roamed around "Heaven",
Not daring to blink, lest we wake,
At Billy Bob's-- Passadena,
The worlds largest club,
Hank's band made the roof rafters shake.

A Countryman's Dream (continued)

In New Orleans we boarded "The Natches"
Mississippi river to ride,
Laid out like a tree in the Everglades,
An Alligator, mouth yawning wide.!

Yes, that place scared the life,
Out of me and Jeannette
A huge snake slithered down from a tree,
Don't let us break down,
Keep this hover-car moving,
Dear Lord, we both prayed fervently.

New York, Washington, Highway one-O- nine
The White House, so fine, so serene,
"Nodding donkeys", Yellow cabs,
And space rockets
Are all things I can now say I've seen

Yes, that trip was great
For me and Jeannette,
A dream world, I still wonder when
Luck's lady, might smile
Perhaps in a while
Dear Lord, Let us go back again.

1990.

It's so hard to believe.

I read in a book of fishes and loaves,
Of water being turned into wine,
How God sent his son, the saviour of man,
To teach us the word and the sign.

Parables, Miracles, and wonderful deeds,
Seas parting to let people through,
Good things that we could, we did 'cos we should
Do to others as they do to you.

But how can I believe there's a God up above,
Who cares for us all as they say,
When suicide terrorists kill, too many to list,
On September Eleventh, Tuesday.

Four planes left the ground, Oblivion bound,
The passengers all unaware,
Of carnage untold about to unfold,
Planned by lunatics hidden somewhere.

Ten minutes into flight, sounds of a fight,
The pilots and crew, overcame,
The planes altered course, no sign of remorse
Flown by killers, who all thought the same.

In uptown New York, folk left home for work,
Not knowing just what lay ahead
The planes rammed the Trade Towers, starting huge fires
Now thousands of people are dead.

It's so hard to believe. (continued)

Two thousand, eight hundred and thirty seven
Innocent victims died,
In a huge holocaust, every single life lost,
As helpless rescuers just stood and cried.

Religious fanatics caused this dreadful deed,
This world is a terrible place,
Osama Bin Laden, the Devil incarnate !!
Enemy of the whole human race.

If good is to prevail,
Lord please do NOT fail,
Stamp out this evil within
As you did long ago, Please give us the sign,
'Cos my faith really is wearing thin.

Yes it's so hard to believe, as you see people grieve,
For atrocities done man to man,
But I guess that I must, in God place my trust,
For IF anyone can, only HE can.
SAVE THE WHOLE HUMAN RACE. !!!!

Dedicated to all those who died......the victims.
        All those who tried....the rescue teams.
        All those who cried....good people, everywhere!!

2002.

To Commemorate the Seventieth Birthday, of my eldest Brother

Arthur. H.A Bassett.
From A.T.C in the 1940's
To S.A.C in the 1950's
To septuagenarian in 2004
Big Brother, that's some journey.

Seventy, But who's counting !!.......

On Saturday, September 25th 2004, we, Jeannette and I were attending the wedding of my niece Emma, the daughter of my sister Peggy, to her fiancé Bryn, which was held at the rather smart venue, "The Monkey Island Hotel", located on a picturesque private island on the Thames, in the village of Bray, near Maidenhead.. We were enjoying a terrific occasion and during the evening reception, dining at the same table as my other niece, Mandy, daughter of eldest brother Arthur.

During a lull in the activities, which was a rare occurrence, Mandy leaned across and said that she was planning a surprise party for her father's 70th birthday, some three months hence. She planned to arrange it for December 19th 2004, Arthur's birthday is actually on the 20th, and would be held at the Masonic Hall in Castleton, a venue I was very familiar with, due to Arthur's involvement with the fraternity, from "way back", and following his support of my application, 1979, I too had become a member of the order in 1980

I had since 1991, been carrying out the duties of caretaker at the aforementioned Hall, and would often receive phone calls from Arthur, and our mutual friend, Peter Duke, to the effect that this function or that event, , would be held at the "Lodge", and that "we would need this done, or the tables set up etc", for what ever the function was, and

I would do whatever the task was. My "involvement" at the Hall was a "God-send" because, since being unable to work, it gave me a purpose, and the Masonic activities were a source of enjoyment from a social angle, for Jeannette and I.

Anyway, back to the story, Mandy asked would Jeannette and I, like to attend her Dad's proposed "bash"---Mandy is a warm, bubbly person, and the moment she asked me, I was only too pleased to accept her invitation, the rest of the evening was most enjoyable, and in due course, we all went our separate ways, and the days passed..........

Since that function back in 2004, Arthur and I have been in each others company on many occasions, at meetings and functions at the Hall, Arthur in his capacity as Bar Manager(Honorary), and me, as a fellow member, chief help, or what-ever, and on these occasions I have always had to be extra careful not to let slip, anything likely to jeopardise Mandy's planned "surprise party", on a number of occasions it has been close to happening, Arthur would say things like"we've got to put the Chapter up" or "don't forget to get this from Peters", and as things continued into December, we would often "run through" the various dates of up coming events in the Hall "calendar".

As December started, it was agreed that "we've got St Mellonius, St Gabriel's, the Carol Service, Oh and Peter wants the Hall for a private "do", on the 19th".........that last statement nearly caught me, a number of times, and the more I thought about it the more worried I became, What if Peter really DID want the venue for a private party? Does Verlie know about Mandy's planned surprise? Is the surprise party a planned surprise for Arthur AND Verlie, —Who can I speak to?, to find out, without letting the cat out of the bag ?.

I knew Mandy lived "up country somewhere", but I couldn't find her phone number anywhere, we have both Julian and Mandy's numbers, but can never find them when we need them, I daren't phone Verlie, for reasons I have already mentioned--------I was in a quandary !!

December is always a busy month at the Masonic Hall, with lots of functions being held at the Hall, —on Saturday the 4th, there were two, a lodge meeting in the morning, and a Golden Wedding celebration, from mid afternoon onwards, on the 7th, another lodge meeting, which was followed by a large Carol Service on Sunday, the 12th, followed by another lodge meeting on Tuesday the 14th, and this was followed by another lodge meeting on Wednesday the15th, --these functions are always a lot more demanding, being Christmas celebrations, and there is always a lot more "debris" to be taken care of due to the nature of the celebrations, decorations, crackers and rubbish aplenty –during all this activity Arthur would ask me to "get some pop" or "get some wine from Peters", or some such request---days were hectic!!

We were at the Hall, the morning following the Wednesday meeting, and Arthur was asking had I seen our brother David, and said that he would be dropping in to see him in the morning, and that he would be going to visit either Julian or Mandy, "Oh and Peter will be having a private "DO" at the Hall on Sunday the 19th, but that would be our lot until the New Year"--I thought, "And that's what you think --Matey !!!".

One evening prior to the 19th, Verlie phoned, and we arranged to meet at the Hall the following morning so that she could explain the table lay-out etc, and Peter also asked me to meet him there to assist with "putting up balloons etc", and this is when my doubting nature "kicked in"--when any event or function "looms near" I tend to wonder just what WILL go wrong or awry?--it rarely ever does, but that's just the way I am, I guess, Oh, I had in the meantime, ascertained that Peter's "do", that Arthur had been telling me about over the past weeks, was, in fact, Mandy's surprise party, , so I knew that it was now "safe" to talk to Verlie too.

On the Saturday, things got rather hectic, Peter, Verlie, Bob and Pat Jayne, and I were all at the Hall, busy doing balloons, Verlie had already shown me her proposed ideas, and last minute plans, and the venue looked great, with the various decorations and references to "70th

Birthday" streamers, etc, —Verlie asked me to put commemorative menus, four to each table of eight diners, and to distribute two red and two white bottles of wine to each table, and that son Julian would be arriving early on the Sunday evening, the day of the party, a table was tactically placed near the entrance from which Julian and I would ensure that the guests would receive welcoming champagne..............

I still didn't really understand how Arthur was being hoodwinked from all the arrangements, but I confirmed that I would be on parade at shortly after six o'clock, on the evening of Sunday the 19th, I was also now confident that with Peter Duke being involved in preparations, things would somehow run smoothly, and this in no way meant that I doubted Verlie's ability at organisation, —it's just that anyone who knows Peter, also knows of his pure determination and organising ability.

At 6.15pm on the night, Jeannette and I duly arrived at the Hall, having travelled by taxi from our home, a number of people were already there, one being Paul Buckner and his daughter, Jessica, —Paul regularly helps behind the bar, there was also another gentleman, who apparently was a musician for the evening, an accomplished key-board player, who had moved our "tactically placed table" away from the entrance......................

Arthur's son Julian arrived with boxes containing various wines and assorted bottles, which gave me something to do......so many on each table, as per Verlie's requests earlier....then Julian said that he was away to take care of something else. Various guests began to arrive and the room began to fill, ...it was now very dark outside and my nerves were beginning to "jangle"---I still didn't know how or when "Big Brother" was coming.

As the minutes passed, Peter arrived and said that Verlie and Mandy, had told Arthur that a meal had been booked at the nearby "Coach and Horses Hotel"...a noted eating house, then Peter said that arrangements had been made for the occupant of the adjoining property to the Hall, The Old Police Station, a working Detective constable named Malcolm

Fairey, would phone Arthur at home, to inform him "that there appeared to be an intruder at the Hall", asking Arthur, the registered "key Holder" to attend to investigate---in the meantime all the vehicles, belonging to the already arrived guests were moved and parked in darkness at the rear of the building---from the outside the place really did look deserted!!

By now the tension and atmosphere was growing, Peter and I were outside, and he phoned Arthur, with words to the effect that we, the lodge, Had had a problem with suspected burglars.......Arthur was on his way up......after what seemed like ages, but was probably only 5 to 10 minutes, or so......from inside we heard the sounds of a vehicle, I was positioned just inside the door, all lights were out, and we waited..........

Peering through a crack in the door, I heard sounds of Arthur and Julian approaching cautiously....they came to the door of the function room and I reached out in the dark, and grabbed Arthur's arm ....the lights went on.... everyone broke into a spontaneous rendition of "Happy Birthday to You" !!!!!!!!!

We pulled Arthur into the room and he was really surprised to see all the familiar faces, I think he was surprised. Somewhat!!!.........After about thirty minutes of casual banter with Arthur circulating amongst the sixty odd guests, we were requested by the chef, Mr Phillip Moles, of "the Huntsman Hotel" Shirenewton, to please take our places at the tables, that dining would proceed forthwith. WE all duly found our named places at the eight large round tables and were served with a delicious soup course, we were then asked to go up in table order, to receive an assorted course of cold meats and salad, coleslaw, and assorted side dishes to which were then added French fries or potatoes, altogether a very tasty and substantial meal, which was followed by a choice of a variety of sweet courses, cheese and biscuits and coffee----altogether an enjoyable meal, having experienced "The Huntsman ", catering quality many times before, I for one was delighted to see that they were our caterers on this auspicious occasion.

After the "eats" were taken care of with much enjoyment by everyone, a "toast" proposal speech was delivered by Arthur's long time friend and golfing companion, Mr Kenny Ware, which contained the expected banter, we have long come to expect from one to the other, on many occasions. Daughter Mandy had earlier in the day said, that she would like me to deliver a piece of verse during the proceedings, but unfortunately she had forgotten to bring it with her, so I can only wonder what the piece was about.

Mandy then delivered a resume of her father's life from his school-days at West Mon, through his National service, and onto his long service at what was originally Cambrian United Dairies at Marshfield to this, his 70th Birthday, --a delightful and often comical tale, which we all enjoyed.

Jeannette and I were sharing a table with brother David, sister Peggy and Alan, Verlie's sister Rita and husband John Purnell and all too soon, it was time to make our Farewells, and head off into the night, and home, ---the last I saw of Arthur, was seeing him balanced precariously on a chair with a huge cigar in one hand, and a "glass of falling down juice" in the other, experiencing great difficulty in remembering just what day it was...................!!!!

In closing I would add that I enjoyed the occasion very much, as did Jeannette, and I am glad that Verlie gave me the opportunity to contribute in some way, to make the occasion the success it really was!!

Arthur, you may be seventy---but don't forget, we old people are only "kids with a lot of experience" !!!!!! SO KEEP ON ROCKING, ... Big Brother !!!

Author's note,

Todays date is May 18th 2010, a Tuesday, he's still rocking and I'm still writing about him !!!

Arthur's Birthday Celebrations (continued)

Relatives and Friends who attended thBirthday celebrations at the Masonic Hall, atleton on Sunday 19ᵗʰ December 2004, Arthur's 70ᵗʰ Birthday which fell on Monday 20ᵗʰ 2004.

Table A
Mr and Mrs Peter Duke
Mr and Mr John Anthony.
Mr and Mrs Christopher Neil.
Mr John Hicks.
Mrs S Dickers.

Table B.
Mr and Mrs Roy Nuth.
Mr and Mrs Graham Rees.
Mr and Mrs R Janes.
Mr and Mrs B Williams.

Table C.
Mr and Mrs John Purnell.
Mr and Mrs Alan Benest.
Mr and Mrs Robert Bassett.
Mr David Bassett.

Table D.
Mr and Mrs G Wilde.
Mr and Mrs D Washbourne.
Mr and Mrs Kenneth Ware.
Mr and Mrs Arthur Bassett.

Table E.
Mr Julian Bassett.
Master Samuel Bassett.
Master Joseph Bassett.
Miss Alice Gilding.
Mr and Mr Ridyard.
Miss Pheobe Ridyard.
Miss Alice Ridyard.

Table F.
Mrs V Suter.
Mrs Carol Gough.
Mr and Mrs Noel Bassett.
Mr and Mrs G Jones.
Mr and Mrs M Lillington.

Table G.
Mr and Mrs D Ford.
Mr L Godwin.
Mr and Mrs G Thomas.
Mr Paul and Sue.

Table H.
Mr and Mrs Anton Attard.
Mr and Mrs Robert Jayne.
Mr and Mrs Harry Williams.
Mr and Mrs Timothy Barry.

Catering arrangements were carried out by Mr Phillip Moles and his staff from "The Huntsman Hotel", Shirenewton, near Chepstow Gwent

A Londoners Guide to the English Language.
"Eastenders" Approved version. C2002.

Marf	: A hole for eating with.
Troof.	: An account of what took place.
Wiv.	: To accompany someone.
Wivart.	: On ones own.
Werf.	: The value of something.
Fanks.	: Sincere gratitude.
Fink.	: To consider.
Geyoows.	: Females.
Ole Biw.	: Police...See Sarn Hiwoo.
Sarmfink.	: Anything.
Ennyfink.	: Something.
Narfink.	: Nothing.
Me Ole Mukkah.	: Friend.
Pukkah.	: Very good
Hev Summa vet	: Try or taste that.
Wosset.	: What is that?.
Nah fanks mite	: No, Thank you sir.
Leve ih aht,	: Forget it.
Brurvah	: A male relative.
Forvah,	: Male parent.
Muvvah,	: Female parent.
Caff,	: Restaurant.
Biby,	: Child.
Orsnoo	: Arsenal
Sarf Wyoos	: An part of Wales.
Vahsow,	: That is all.
Gown darn,	: Put into prison.
Furvah,	: Further away.

Snart,	: Carrier of tales,
A marny geezer,	: A wealthy man.
Wossarp,	: What is wrong?
Geh vat darn yer neck,	: Drink that.
Shah tit,	: Please be quiet.
Gihdorf,	: Please go away.
Nar ya plice,	: Dont show off.
Mowhar,	: Car.
Ars ya forvah,	: Sex.
Nawoo,	: No.
Sarn hiwoo,	: Sun Hill, See ITV's "The Bill".
Cuhant,	: Could not.
Sceoo	: School.
Darn a pab,	: In public house.
Bow rice,	: A porting event between the University's
Wos gahwin on,	: What is happening?
Unchur,	: Aren't you.?
Me Missiz as goh ve armp	: My wife isn't happy.
Neh moynd ay?	: Don't worry.

Thoughts of a simple man!!!

Always remember, If you can keep your head whilst all those around you, are panicking and losing theirs, ----By the end of the day, you'll be almost a foot taller than them

Recitation.
Haf a litre of dri-pfhennig rice,
Haf a litre of treecull
Das ist ve way the money has vent
Poppink is going the veezells!!!

You'll never believe it, but when I was young, I was ugly !!

If at first you don't succeed, ...Sod it, Pack it in.

The early bird catches the worm,
But it's the second mouse that eats the cheese !!.......Think about it!!!

They say that Heavens a wonderful place,
Angels are painted with smiles on each face,
There's just one question, Please tell me why?
If it's so "blinkin"good, Why're we all scared to die??

Summary

Today is May 20th 2010, and this IS the last page of my manuscript, which I started writing in 1996, there has been many "finished " copies, given to various family members, which probably eventually found the way into the nearest dustbin, but over the interceding years during moments of contemplation, memories have surfaced and gain inclusion into this ongoing collection, but I am now 71 years old and my main ambition is to "see my efforts in print", and to that end I have put myself into the hands of an "on-line" publishing company Authorhouse, of Milton Keynes, England and in order to make use of their facilities, I needed to transfer my manuscript back ONTO an electronic copy document in order to transfer it to the publishers, on line.

This is completely unknown territory for me and if successful will have saved me a lot of money, I have already received an offer of publication as shown in the beginning of my manuscript,

As stated earlier many copies have probably found their way into dustbins throughout the area, but they were only rough and unfinished ones, this is the only completed document and will remain in my possession, and is the only one I consider completed to the best of my ability and memory, I have enjoyed writing and seeing it take shape, There are at this juncture many photos which I have to get to the required standard for acceptance by the publishers, which I have personally enlarged and printed myself, which have been compiled into an Album in my possession, which will maybe prove helpful to any of this family, should they ever attempt to do research on the Bassett name in years to come.

It is now Christmas Eve 2010 and during the past year I have been beavering away, putting this manuscript in some semblance of order with the intention of getting it published by Authorhouse Ltd a company based in America, I have also joined "The Alcan Singers" a small male voice choir based in Rogerstone, just outside Newport consisting of mostly ex Alcan Industries employees, who are actually lads I grew up with in my teens who were mentioned in earlier chapters, and in the aforementioned "The Rogerstone Boys" poem, so the wheel has turned full circle

Robert W.M. Bassett.
Thursday 20ᵗʰ May 2010.

:

THE END.